The French Revoluti
c1780–99

By Alex Kerr

Complete Book: First edition

"As custodians of history, we have a sacred duty to preserve the stories of the forgotten, to give voice to the marginalized, and to ensure their struggles are not in vain."

Max Robespierre

Preface:

This book intends to give as much information as possible about the history of the French Revolution and the rise of Napoleon and relate it to the IGCSE Edexcel Exam Board.

Alex Kerr has been teaching History and Politics for over a decade. He is a graduate of Oxford Brookes University and has completed a PGCE at the Institute of Education, London as well as completing courses at the Johann Cruyff Institute, Barcelona.

This book will cover:

1. The Origins of the Revolution, c1780–87

2. Short-term causes of the Revolution: from Assembly of Notables to Estates General, 1787–89

3. Developments 1789–92

4. Convention and Terror, 1792–94

5. Directory and First Consul – the fall of Robespierre to the Rise of Napoleon, 1794–99

The exam paper is divided into three questions.

It is also divided into three question types:

(a): Wants the student to analyse a source or extract related to the French Revolution.

(b): Explain two effects of an event that took place during the French Revolution.

(c): Analysis of a statement and look at both sides of an argument. The answer is to be written with an introduction, a main body, and a conclusion.

Coming Soon

There will be a supplemental book to this one, with ideas and questions on how to approach the exam.

Chapter 1 The Origins of the Revolution, c1780–87

The long-term causes the influence of the Enlightenment. The impact in France of involvement in the American War of Independence. The Three Estates – their duties and privileges. The role of Louis XVI. The unpopularity of Marie Antoinette. The reasons for and extent of financial problems. Policies of Necker, the problem of poor harvests.

Chapter 2 Short-term causes of the Revolution: from Assembly of Notables to Estates General, 1787–89

The short-term causes: the Assembly of Notables (1787). the policies of Calonne and Brienne and their consequences. the key events of 1789 and their causes and consequences. including the meeting of the Estates General, the Tennis Court Oath, the storming of the Bastille, the Grande Peur, and the setting up of the National Assembly.

Chapter 3 Developments 1789–92

Changes brought about by the Constituent Assembly (1789–91). the flight to Varennes and its impact. the roles of the Sans Culottes, Girondins and Jacobins. the Legislative Assembly (1791–92). the declaration of war on Austria and Prussia and its impact, the reasons for the coup of August 1792, and the setting up of the National Convention.

Chapter 4 Convention and Terror, 1792–94

The National Convention, the Edict of Fraternity. The Trial and Execution of Louis XVI. The work of the Committee of Public Safety. The elimination of the Girondins. The role of Robespierre. The reason for and impact of the Terror.

Chapter 5 Directory and First Consul – the fall of Robespierre to the Rise of Napoleon, 1794–99

Reasons for Robespierre's downfall and execution. The Thermidorian Reaction, the White Terror; the setting up of the Directory, its limitations, and achievements. The royalist challenge and the coup of 18 Fructidor. The reasons for the fall of the Directory; Napoleon Bonaparte was named "First Consul." Achievements of the Revolution in France (1789–99).

Table of Contents

Table of Contents...iv

Let's Get Started!...6

Glossary for French Revolution 7

Key People of the French Revolution..9

Timeline 11

Chapter One: The Origins of the Revolution, c1780–87 14

Long-Term Causes: The Enlightenment...14

Long-Term Causes: The American Revolution..15

Long-term Causes: The Three Estates 17

Long-Term Causes: the unpopularity of Marie Antoinette..............................22

Long-Term Causes: the reasons for and extent of financial problems 25

Long-Term Causes: the policies of Necker 28

Long Term Causes: the problem of poor harvests. 30

Chapter Two: Short-term Causes of the Revolution:....................................31

The Assembly of Notables (1787) 32

The policies of Calonne and Brienne and their consequences..........................33

The Tennis Court Oath...34

The storming of the Bastille...35

The Grande Peur 36

The creation of the National Assembly 36

Chapter Three: Developments 1789–92 37

Changes brought about by the Constituent Assembly (1789–91), ...37

The flight to Varennes and its impact...38

The roles of the Sans Culottes, Girondins and Jacobins..................................40

The Legislative Assembly (1791–92)...41

The declaration of war on Austria and Prussia and its impact..........................42

The reasons for the coup of August 1792 43

Setting up of the National Convention...43

Chapter Four: Convention and Terror, 1792–94...45

The National Convention...45

The Edict of Fraternity...46

The Trial and Execution of Louis XVI...47

The work of the Committee of Public Safety 48

The elimination of the Girondins..50

The Role of Robespierre & The Reason for and Impact of the Terror 51

    Chapter Five: Directory and First Consul – the fall of Robespierre to the Rise
of Napoleon, 1794–99...54

Reasons for Robespierre's downfall and execution...54

The Thermidorian Reaction 55

The White Terror 56

The setting up of the Directory, its limitations, and achievements......................57

The royalist challenge and the coup of 18 Fructidor 59

The Reasons for the Fall of the Directory..60

Napoleon Bonaparte named "First Consul."..61

Achievements of the Revolution in France (1789–99) 62

Epilogue/Conclusion...64

Bibliography 65

Let's Get Started!

1. When you think of France, what do you think of?

2. Have you heard about Napoleon, Max Robespierre, Marie Antoinette?

3. Have you heard about the Louvre or the Mona Lisa?

4. Have you visited Versailles or Paris?

5. What is the significance of France today?

6. What was the political background and government of France in 1799?

In 1792, France became engulfed in a series of conflicts with foreign powers, leading to the overthrow of the monarchy and the establishment of the First French Republic. During this period, the Tricolour flag, with its iconic blue, white, and red stripes, emerged as the national symbol of France.

The blue and red colours were taken from the city of Paris, while the white symbolized the monarchy. However, after the revolutionaries abolished the monarchy, the tricolour came to represent the ideals of the revolution itself.

Before the French Revolution, life in France was a tapestry woven with threads of opulence and inequality. The monarchy reigned supreme, with King Louis XVI and his queen, Marie Antoinette, residing in the grandeur of Versailles. Yet beneath the mask of lavishness, a simmering discontent brewed among the common people who faced social and economic hardships.

It was during this time that figures like Maximilien Robespierre emerged. Robespierre, a passionate advocate for justice, recognized the power of history in shaping the future. He believed that studying the past could unearth the mechanisms of oppression and inspire a pursuit of a fairer society. The French Revolution became a turning point, an opportunity for the oppressed to challenge the established order and demand their rights. The revolutionaries rallied around ideals of liberty, equality, and fraternity, forever altering the course of France and, indeed, the world.

Today, France stands as a testament to the enduring legacy of this pivotal moment in history. From the iconic Louvre Museum, housing treasures like the enigmatic Mona Lisa, to the enduring allure of Paris, and being one of the leading lights of the European Union, this nation continues to inspire and captivate.

But to truly comprehend the significance of modern-day France, we must journey back to its roots. So, fasten your seatbelts, dear IGCSE history students, for an exhilarating expedition awaits. Together, we shall unravel the secrets of the past and discover the true essence of France's remarkable journey.

Glossary for French Revolution

Monarchy: A form of government where the supreme power is vested in a single individual, usually a hereditary ruler, who holds the title of king or queen and exercises authority over a state or territory.

Guillotine: A device used for carrying out capital punishment by decapitation.

Committee of Public Safety: A governing body established during the French Revolution in 1793. It was responsible for the defence of the revolution, managing the war effort, and maintaining internal security. Led by Maximilien Robespierre.

Reign of Terror: A period of radical violence and state-sanctioned repression that occurred during the French Revolution from 1793 to 1794.

Revolution: A fundamental and often abrupt change in political, social, or economic systems, typically occurring through a popular uprising or resistance against established authority.

Ancien Régime: Refers to the traditional social and political system that prevailed in France before the French Revolution, characterized by an absolute monarchy, a rigid social hierarchy, and privileged status for the aristocracy and clergy.

Absolute Monarchy: A form of government where a single ruler, typically a king or queen, possesses complete and unrestricted power, usually inherited through a hereditary line, without any checks or balances imposed by other branches of government or constitutional limitations.

Real Wages: The actual purchasing power of wages earned by workers, considering the effects of inflation and changes in the cost of living. Real wages reflect the ability of workers to afford goods and services based on their income relative to the prevailing prices of goods.

Empirical Evidence: Information or data derived from observation, experimentation, or real-world experiences. Empirical evidence serves as the basis for scientific research, allowing researchers to draw conclusions and make claims supported by objective data.

Social Mobility: The ability of individuals or groups to move up or down the social ladder in terms of their socioeconomic status. Social mobility can occur through factors such as education, occupational opportunities, and economic changes, and it is often seen as a measure of societal openness and fairness.

Compte Rendu: A French term meaning "report" or "account." It refers to a written or oral summary or record of a meeting, event, or activity, providing a detailed overview or analysis of the proceedings or outcomes.

Levee en Masse, Conscription: Levee en masse refers to a mass mobilization of the population, often involving conscription or the compulsory enlistment of citizens into military service. It was a policy implemented during the French Revolution to create a large and active army by drafting men from all social classes.

Council of Five Hundred: A legislative body established during the French Revolution in 1795. Comprised of 500 members, it served as the lower house of the French government, participating in the legislative process and proposing laws and policies.

The Council of Ancients was one of the two legislative bodies established during the French Revolution. Composed of elder statesmen, it held the power to review and approve or reject legislation proposed by the Council of Five Hundred, providing a moderating influence on the revolutionary government.

Key People of the French Revolution

King Louis XVI

The last Bourbon king of France, whose reign witnessed the eruption of the revolution and ultimately led to his execution.

Marie Antoinette

The queen of France and wife of Louis XVI, whose extravagant lifestyle and perceived indifference to the suffering of the French people made her a symbol of royal excess.

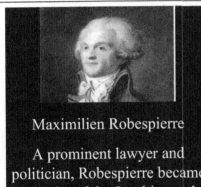

Maximilien Robespierre

A prominent lawyer and politician, Robespierre became a leader of the Jacobins and played a key role in the Reign of Terror, advocating for radical revolutionary measures.

Jean-Paul Marat

A journalist and political theorist, Marat was a vocal supporter of the revolution and used his newspaper to advocate for violence against perceived enemies of the revolution.

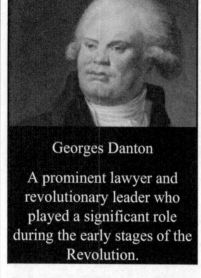

Georges Danton

A prominent lawyer and revolutionary leader who played a significant role during the early stages of the Revolution.

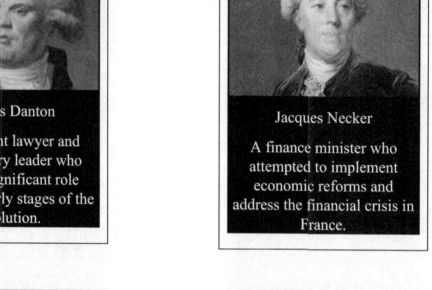

Jacques Necker

A finance minister who attempted to implement economic reforms and address the financial crisis in France.

Charlotte Corday

A Girondin sympathizer who assassinated Jean-Paul Marat, believing it would stop the violence and restore peace.

Napoleon Bonaparte

A military general who rose to power after the Revolution and eventually became the Emperor of France.

Timeline

Some key moments in the French Revolution, 1789- 1794

Year	Date	Event	Government
1789	January 24	Louis XVI summons the Estates General	Monarchy
	May 5	Estates General convenes	
	June 17	The deputies of the Third Estate declared themselves the National Assembly	National Assembly
	June 20	The "Tennis Court Oath"	
	July 9	The National Assembly reconstitutes itself as the National Constituent Assembly	National Constituent Assembly
	July 11	Louis dismisses Necker, a popular minister	
	July 14	Storming of the Bastille	
	August 4	Abolition of feudal (noble, clerical) rights	
	August 26	Declaration of the Rights of Man	
	October 5-6	The Wives' March; Louis "kidnapped" back to Paris	
1790	May 19	National Assembly abolishes the nobility	
	July 12	Civil Constitution of the French Clergy	
	November 27	Clergy instructed to swear allegiance to France	
1791	March 10	Pope Pius VI condemns the Civil Constitution of the Clergy	
	June 20-21	Louis & Marie Antoinette flee; captured at Varennes	
	August 27	Declaration of Pillnitz: Austria & Prussia express support for Louis	

	September	New Constitution was ratified (with the support of Louis)	
	September 30	Last day of the National Constituent Assembly	
	October 1	The first session of the new National Legislative Assembly	Legislative Assembly
1792	April 20	France declares war on Austria	
	April 25	The first use of a guillotine	
	June 13	Prussia declares war on France	
	August 9	Paris Commune established	
	August 10	Parisians storm Tuileries palace; end of Louis XVI's power	
	September 20	French cannons drive back Prussians at Valmy	
	September 20	The newly elected National Convention holds its first session	National Convention
	September 21	The French Republic proclaimed	
1793	January 21	Louis XVI executed	
	February 1	France declares war on Britain and Netherlands	
	April 6	The Committee of Public Safety founded	
	June 24	New Constitution proclaimed	
	August 12	Mass conscription instituted	
	October 5	Republican calendar adopted	
	October 16	Marie Antoinette executed	
	December 19	British leave Toulon, following a successful military operation led by Napoleon Bonaparte	
1794	June 8	Festival of the Supreme Being	

	July 28	Robespierre guillotined	
	July	Reign of Terror Ends	
1795	August 22	New Constitution: Directory Takes Power	Directory
	October 5	Napoleon defeats a Royalist Mob in Paris	
1796	March 2	Bonaparte was made commander of the Army of Italy	
	April 7	After a series of victories by Bonaparte, the Austrians agreed to negotiate.	
1798	July 1–2	Bonaparte lands in Egypt	
	July 21	Bonaparte defeats the Mameluks at the Battle of the Pyramids.	
1799	March 7	Bonaparte captures Jaffa in Palestine. Some of his soldiers are infected with the plague.	
	October 9	Bonaparte returns to France.	
	October 16	Bonaparte arrives in Paris for public celebrations.	
	November 9	Napoleon leads a coup d'état taking power between himself and two others.	
	December 24	Bonaparte is made First Consul Traditional histories mark this date as the end of the French Revolution.	Napoleon

Chapter One: The Origins of the Revolution, c1780–87

Ask yourself:

1. Should one family have more power or rights than any other?

2. Would you want a Monarchy today?

3. Should a religious group have political power?

Liberty Leading the People (1830)
by Eugene Delacroix

Long-Term Causes: The Enlightenment

"Humour is the philosopher's sword, cutting through the armour of tyranny with wit and ridicule." - Denis Diderot

The Enlightenment, a philosophical and intellectual movement that swept through Europe during the 18th century, played a significant role as a long-term cause of the French Revolution. It emerged as a response to the prevailing feudal and absolutist systems, challenging traditional authority and advocating for reason, individual liberty, and equality. The ideas generated during the Enlightenment period laid the intellectual groundwork for the revolutionary feeling that engulfed France.

Enlightened thinkers, such as Voltaire, Rousseau, and Montesquieu, questioned the existing social order and advocated for the concepts of liberty, equality, and reason. One of the fundamental concepts promoted by Enlightenment thinkers was the belief in the sovereignty of the people. They challenged the divine right of kings and argued that political power should derive from the consent of the governed. Thinkers like John Locke and Jean-Jacques Rousseau emphasized the idea of popular sovereignty and the social contract, asserting that governments should serve the interests of the people and protect their natural rights.

Furthermore, the Enlightenment challenged religious authority and promoted secularism. Philosophers like Voltaire advocated for religious tolerance and the separation of church and state, challenging the power and influence of the Catholic Church in France. The Enlightenment thinkers emphasized the importance of reason, scientific inquiry, and empirical evidence, questioning traditional religious beliefs and superstitions.

One key aspect of the Enlightenment that contributed to the French Revolution was the emphasis on individual rights and the concept of natural law. Enlightenment philosophers argued that all individuals possessed inherent rights, such as the right to life, liberty, and property. These ideas directly challenged the absolute authority of the monarchy and the privileges enjoyed by the aristocracy. The notion that power should be derived from the consent of the governed resonated deeply with the oppressed and marginalized sections of French society, who yearned for greater political participation and representation.

Moreover, the Enlightenment promoted the importance of reason and critical thinking. Intellectuals during this period advocated for the application of reason in all aspects of life, including politics and governance. This emphasis on rationality fostered a spirit of questioning and a desire for reform. People began to question the arbitrary and unfair practices of the monarchy and sought to replace them with a system that was based on reason and justice.

Another significant contribution of the Enlightenment to the French Revolution was the spread of new ideas through literature, pamphlets, and salons. The dissemination of these ideas led to a growing sense of political consciousness among the masses. Ordinary people began to engage in political debates, questioning the legitimacy of the existing social hierarchy and demanding greater social equality.

The Enlightenment also played a role in exposing the corruption and abuses of the Ancien Régime. Enlightened thinkers criticized the extravagant lifestyle of the monarchy and the clergy, the oppressive taxation system, and the lack of social mobility. These critiques further fuelled the discontent that eventually erupted into revolutionary fervour.

In summary, the Enlightenment had a lasting impact on the causes of the French Revolution. It fostered the growth of ideas centred around individual rights, reason, and equality. These ideas inspired a generation of French citizens to question and challenge the existing social and political order. The intellectual and philosophical foundations laid during the Enlightenment helped shape the aspirations of the revolutionaries and provided the ideological framework for the transformative events that unfolded during the French Revolution.

Long-Term Causes: The American Revolution

American General Washington Crossing the Delaware, an 1851 painting by Emanuel Leutze

A significant influence on the Revolution was the successful American Revolution that unfolded across the Atlantic. The American Revolution, which culminated in the United States gaining independence from Britain, served as a powerful inspiration for the French people. It showcased the potential of ordinary citizens to rise against an oppressive monarchy and achieve political freedom.

The American Revolution demonstrated that ideas of liberty, equality, and popular sovereignty could be put into practice, fuelling the aspirations of the French populace. The French intellectuals and philosophers, influenced by Enlightenment ideas, found resonance in the principles of the American Revolution, such as the notion of individual rights and the social contract between the government and the governed.

France's involvement in the American Revolution was fuelled by their desire to weaken their longtime rival, Britain. In fact, the French government secretly spent approximately 1.3 billion livres (that's roughly $39 Billion in today's money) supporting the American cause. That's one expensive friendship!

France's involvement in the American Revolution further deepened the impact of this transatlantic inspiration. The French monarchy's decision to support the American colonists against their common rival, Britain, strained the already fragile French economy. The financial burden of financing the war effort, along with the extravagant lifestyle of the monarchy and the nobility, exacerbated the economic crisis in France.

The military involvement in America also exposed French soldiers to revolutionary ideas, as they witnessed the fight for freedom and the power of a people united against tyranny. Upon returning to France, these soldiers became potential agents of change, sharing their experiences and ideals, further igniting the spirit of revolution.

Moreover, the French monarchy's support for the American Revolution led to a substantial increase in the national debt, which exacerbated France's financial instability. The growing economic crisis created discontent among the population, particularly the urban and rural poor who bore the brunt of taxation while the nobility enjoyed privileges and exemptions.

The American Revolution inspired other nations around the world to seek their own independence. The revolution's success and the ideals of liberty and equality it championed echoed throughout history, igniting similar movements in countries like Haiti, and Latin American colonies. The ripple effect of revolution!

Thus, the American Revolution and France's involvement therein acted as long-term causes of the French Revolution. They inspired the French people with the notion of challenging the established order, provided a practical example of revolutionary ideals in action, and had a considerable impact on their finances. The cost of their involvement, combined with a struggling economy and excessive royal spending, contributed to France's mounting debt crisis.

The revolutionary spirit, combined with the socio-economic grievances and the intellectual climate of the Enlightenment, set the stage for the monumental events that would unfold during the French Revolution. It was like a financial domino effect!

Long-term Causes: The Three Estates

What's going on in this picture?

A FAUT ESPERER Q'EU[*]JEU LA FINIRA BEN TOT

Cartoon showing the Third Estate carrying the weight of the clergy and the nobility (1789)

The influence of the Three Estates and their respective duties and privileges played a significant role as long-term causes of the French Revolution. In the social structure of pre-revolutionary France, society was divided into three main groups known as estates.

First Estate

The First Estate consisted of the clergy, which included bishops, priests, and other church officials. They enjoyed immense privileges, including exemption from many taxes and the ability to collect tithes from the common people. The clergy held vast land and wealth, which contributed to their power and influence. However, their wealth and privileged status led to resentment among the lower classes who were burdened with heavy taxes.

Step right up, history enthusiasts, for a dose of mind-boggling facts about the First Estate and their mind-boggling privileges during the French Revolution! Get ready to delve into the wacky world of the clergy and their exemptions, which played a role in fuelling the flames of revolution.

Fact #1: Tax-Free Status Extravaganza!

Imagine a world where you pay no taxes while your fellow citizens shoulder the burden. Well, that's precisely what the First Estate, comprised of the clergy, enjoyed. They basked in the glory of tax exemptions, leaving the common folk to fund the kingdom's needs. No wonder the taxpaying masses started to get a little miffed!

Fact #2: The Tithe!

Hold onto your hats, folks, because the clergy had a unique way of collecting their version of pocket money. Known as tithes, these were mandatory payments made by the peasantry to the Church. But guess what? The clergy themselves were exempt from paying tithes! They gleefully collected the fruits of their followers' labour while keeping their own pockets lined with their hard-earned dough.

Fact #3: The Nifty Privilege of Imprisoning!

Ever wished you could be a law unto yourself? Well, the First Estate had that power! Clergymen could arrest and imprison anyone they deemed a threat to their divine authority. Talk about a get-out-of-jail-free card! It's no wonder the clergy started rubbing some folks the wrong way.

Fact #4: No Heavy Lifting for Holy Folks!

Do you know those irritating tasks like serving in the military or performing manual labour? Well, the clergy had a get-out-of-work-free card! They were exempt from military service and the drudgery of physical labour, leaving those burdens for the commoners to bear. It's no surprise that resentment and discontent started brewing among the hardworking masses.

Second Estate

The Second Estate comprised the nobility, which included the aristocracy, landowners, and the royal family. Like the clergy, the nobility held significant power and wealth. They were exempt from many taxes and enjoyed feudal privileges such as hunting rights and collecting dues from the peasants who worked their lands. The nobility also occupied important positions in the government, military, and courts. However, their privileges and exploitation of the lower classes created a sense of injustice and inequality.

Fact #1: No Taxes!

The Second Estate, composed of the noble class, managed to avoid the burdens of paying taxes that ordinary citizens had to bear. Yes, you heard it right! They skipped out on contributing their fair share to the state's finances, leaving the burden to fall heavily on the Third Estate.

Exemption 1: Tax Houdini's - The noble Second Estate managed to magically escape paying direct taxes, such as the dreaded taille. While ordinary folks were weighed down by tax burdens, the nobles waltzed through life tax-free. It's like they had a secret "No Tax" spell!

Exemption 2: Funky Financial Feats - Brace yourselves for this one! The Second Estate not only avoided direct taxes but also waved goodbye to taxes on land and property. Picture vast estates and lavish manors sitting there, free from any financial obligations. It's enough to make your jaw drop!

Exemption 3: Snubbing the Salt Tax - Salt was once a highly taxed commodity, but guess who managed to evade this salty burden? That's right, the Second Estate! They could sprinkle salt on their meals without worrying about the hefty tax that commoners had to pay.

Exemption 4: Skipping the Stampede - Stamp duty was another burden dodged by the noble elite. While regular citizens had to pay taxes on various official documents and paperwork, the Second Estate could flaunt their fancy parchments without ever touching their pockets. They were certainly stampede-free!

Exemption 5: Bye-Bye to the Barn Tax - Imagine not having to contribute a single centime towards maintaining public buildings like barns. Well, that's exactly what the Second Estate enjoyed! While peasants toiled away, the nobles didn't have to lift a finger or open their wallets. Talk about barn envy!

Exemption 6: Tax-Free Tithes - The nobles dared to avoid paying tithes, a percentage of their income that was traditionally contributed to the Church. While commoners faithfully fulfilled their religious duties, the Second Estate conveniently sidestepped this obligation.

Fact #2: No Military Service!

Picture this: the noble elite of the Second Estate were not obliged to serve in the military. While commoners risked their lives on the battlefield, these privileged nobles could sit back and sip their fancy wines, avoiding any duty to defend their nation.

Fact #3: No Obligations!

The noble class had the extraordinary privilege of being exempt from numerous feudal obligations, such as the duty to maintain public infrastructure and contribute to the well-being of their communities. They were essentially living in a world where obligations were optional!

Fact #4: Hunting Anyone?

Well, the nobles of the Second Estate had exclusive rights to hunt on vast stretches of land, often referred to as "Royal Forests." This meant that even if starving, commoners could face severe punishment for hunting game to feed their families.

Fact #5: Legally Protected

The Second Estate was also granted special judicial privileges. They were subjected to their legal system, separate from the laws that applied to the rest of the population. This meant that nobles often received lenient sentences or even escaped punishment altogether, regardless of their actions.

Fact #6: Money Makers

Get ready for an unbelievable fact: the nobles dared to demand feudal dues from the peasants who worked their lands. These dues often included excessive taxes, forced labour, and even the right to collect tolls on roads. It was a never-ending cycle of exploitation!

Third Estate

The Third Estate represented most of the population, including commoners, peasants, urban workers, and the bourgeoisie (middle class). This estate bore the burden of heavy taxation, including the hated taille (land tax), along with feudal obligations to the nobility. They faced economic hardships, poverty, and limited social mobility, while the privileged classes enjoyed wealth and influence. The Third Estate also resented the lack of political representation, as decisions were often made by the king and the privileged classes without their input.

Obligation 1: Corvée Labour – The Third Estate had the dubious honour of being responsible for unpaid forced labour. Picture this: while the nobles lounged in luxury, the peasants toiled away, repairing roads and maintaining infrastructure without receiving a single sou in return. It was a never-ending cycle of back-breaking labour!

Obligation 2: Banalités – Hold on tight, because here comes a jaw-dropping obligation! The Third Estate was subjected to the whims of the Second Estate's bread ovens, mills, and wine presses. Peasants were forced to pay exorbitant fees to use these facilities, leaving them with little choice but to line the pockets of the privileged nobility.

Obligation 3: Taille Taxes – Brace yourselves for a taxing fact! The Third Estate was burdened with the heaviest tax of them all – the taille. While the nobles danced at lavish balls and revelled in their riches, the commoners had no choice but to open their wallets and endure this crushing burden on their hard-earned income.

Obligation 4: Feudal Dues – Prepare to be flabbergasted by this outrageous obligation! The Third Estate was at the mercy of the Second Estate, forced to pay excessive feudal dues. These dues often included exorbitant taxes, tithes, and fees, leaving the commoners struggling to make ends meet while the nobles lived in opulence.

Obligation 5: Game Laws – Hold onto your hats, because this obligation is truly hair-raising! The Third Estate faced severe penalties for hunting game on the lands of the Second Estate. While the noble elite indulged in lavish hunting parties, the commoners risked imprisonment or even death for daring to put food on their tables. Talk about an unfair advantage!

Obligation 6: Seigneurial Justice – Get ready for an astonishing fact! The Third Estate had the unfortunate privilege of being subjected to the whims of the Seigneurial Courts, controlled by the noble class. Justice was often biased and unjust, with the commoners facing severe punishments while the nobles enjoyed preferential treatment and lenient sentences.

These stark social inequalities and the discontent among the Third Estate were catalysts for the French Revolution. The privileged classes enjoyed immense privileges and wealth while the common people struggled to make ends meet. The burden of taxation and feudal obligations weighed heavily on the lower classes, leading to grievances and demands for reform.

The call for equality and social justice became a central theme during the Revolution, with the Third Estate demanding representation and an end to the privileges of the clergy and nobility. The grievances and frustrations of the Third Estate would eventually ignite the flames of the revolution, culminating in the storming of the Bastille in 1789.

In summary, the influence of the Three Estates and their duties and privileges served as long-term causes of the French Revolution. The stark social inequalities, economic disparities, and lack of political representation endured by the Third Estate fuelled discontent and the demand for change. The Revolution aimed to overthrow the privilege and power held by the clergy and nobility, and usher in a new era of equality and justice.

Long-Term Causes: King Louis XVI

Portrait of Louis XVI by Antoine-François Callet, 1779

The influence of Louis XVI as a long-term cause of the French Revolution cannot be underestimated. As the last Bourbon king of France, Louis XVI inherited a nation burdened with economic and social crises, and his reign exacerbated the existing tensions that ultimately led to the eruption of the revolution. Louis XVI's personal characteristics, political decisions, and inability to effectively address the challenges facing France played a significant role in shaping the discontent that fuelled the revolution.

"The King's vacillating nature has rendered him ineffective as a leader, causing a loss of faith in the monarchy among the people." - Marie Antoinette's confidante, Madame Campan, 1792.

First and foremost, Louis XVI's indecisiveness and lack of strong leadership proved detrimental to his reign. He was known for his indecisiveness and hesitancy in making crucial decisions, which created a sense of uncertainty and a lack of direction in the government. This lack of firm leadership undermined the monarchy's authority and fuelled growing dissatisfaction among the French people.

> "*The King's hesitation and lack of leadership in addressing the financial crisis have only deepened the nation's unrest.*" - Memoirs of the Duc de Liancourt, 1789.

Furthermore, Louis XVI's extravagant lifestyle and the lavish spending of the royal court contributed to the financial crisis that plagued France.

Personal Expenses: Louis XVI had a penchant for luxury and indulgence. His expenses, including lavish clothing, fine dining, and extravagant parties, amounted to an average of 6 million livres per year.

Royal Court Expenditures: The courtiers surrounding the king were also known for their extravagant lifestyles. The annual cost of maintaining the court, including salaries, pensions, and allowances, reached approximately 12 million livres.

This would be about £300 million a year in today's money!

The monarchy's heavy reliance on borrowing, combined with the immense debt inherited from previous reigns, exacerbated the economic hardships faced by the common people. While Louis XVI attempted some economic reforms, his efforts were overshadowed by his inability to effectively implement them or make the necessary sacrifices himself.

Louis XVI's political decisions also drove discontent and resentment. He resisted calls for political reform and was hesitant to grant the demands of the Third Estate, which represented most of the French population. This resistance to change and his perceived indifference to the struggles of the common people intensified the grievances against the monarchy and laid the groundwork for revolutionary sentiments.

Moreover, Louis XVI's mishandling of the Estates-General, the representative assembly, further alienated the people and deepened the crisis. His failure to effectively address the grievances and demands put forth by the Third Estate led to the formation of the National Assembly and the subsequent storming of the Bastille, marking a pivotal moment in the French Revolution.

In summary, Louis XVI's reign as the king of France played a significant role in the long-term causes of the French Revolution. His indecisiveness, lavish lifestyle, resistance to change, and mishandling of political affairs contributed to the deepening discontent and grievances among the French population. These factors, combined with the existing economic and social crises, laid the foundation for the revolutionary movement that sought to challenge the authority and power of the monarchy. Louis XVI's actions, or lack thereof, ultimately set the stage for the dramatic events that would reshape the course of French history.

We didn't tell you everything about the Royal spending…

Long-Term Causes: the unpopularity of Marie Antoinette

Marie Antoinette, the queen consort of France, undeniably played a significant role in the long-term causes that ultimately led to the French Revolution. Her influence and actions, often viewed as representative of the monarchy's detachment and extravagance, contributed to the growing discontent and resentment among the French population.

> What do you think of Marie Antoinette's hair style for a ball?

Marie Antoinette, an Austrian princess, married the French King Louis XVI at a young age. Her foreign origins and the lavish lifestyle she embraced were subject to intense scrutiny and criticism from the French public. The queen's extravagant spending and indulgence in luxury earned her the reputation of being out of touch with the realities faced by most of the French people.

The image of Marie Antoinette as a symbol of excess and privilege was perpetuated by her lavish spending at a time when France was grappling with severe economic hardships. As France faced mounting financial crises, exacerbated by the cost of wars and the extravagant court lifestyle, the queen's extravagant spending only fuelled public anger and exacerbated social inequality.

Lavish Palace of Versailles: Marie Antoinette and the royal court resided in the opulent Palace of Versailles, which was an emblem of luxury and excess. The cost of maintaining the palace was exorbitant, accounting for about 6% of the annual state budget at the time. We will talk more about the Palace later on…

Extravagant Personal Wardrobe: Marie Antoinette was renowned for her extravagant fashion choices and lavish personal wardrobe. It is estimated that she spent approximately 1.5 million livres (French currency) on clothing and accessories each year, which was a significant sum given the financial strain on the country.

An Heir:

Marie Antoinette's failure to produce an heir to the French throne had significant repercussions on the reputation of the royal family and played a notable role in fuelling the sentiments that led to the French Revolution. As the queen of France, her primary duty was to secure the continuation of the dynasty, and her inability to bear children was seen as a personal failing. This perceived weakness in fulfilling her maternal role was seized upon by her critics, who used it to portray her as frivolous, selfish, and disconnected from the struggles of the common people. The absence of an heir also fuelled uncertainty and instability within the monarchy, as it raised concerns about a potential succession crisis. This situation further eroded public trust in the royal family, contributing to the growing discontent that ultimately erupted in the French Revolution.

Hameau de la Reine (Queen's Hamlet):

What do you think?

Marie Antoinette had a personal retreat called the Hameau de la Reine, a picturesque village constructed within the grounds of Versailles. This whimsical retreat, complete with working farmhouses and a lake, cost around 1.6 million livres to build, adding to the financial burden.

Gambling and Court Entertainment: The royal court was known for its extravagant parties, balls, and gambling. Marie Antoinette herself had a fondness for gambling and spent large sums on her gambling activities. In 1777 alone, she lost approximately 1.5 million livres playing cards.

Affinity for Jewels and Decorations: Marie Antoinette had a fascination with jewellery and frequently acquired expensive gems and ornaments. One of the most notable examples was the purchase of the extravagant "Diamond Necklace Affair," which cost an astounding 1.6 million livres. Although she never actually purchased the necklace, the scandal and associated debt tarnished her reputation.

Adding up the figures mentioned in the previous examples, the total cost of livres attributed to Marie Antoinette's extravagant lifestyle and the lavish spending of the royal court is estimated to be around 6.2 million livres.

Today that would be $46.5 million, a year!

Rumours of political interference:

Furthermore, Marie Antoinette's perceived interference in politics and her association with influential court factions strained her relationship with the public. She was accused of exerting undue influence on her husband, King Louis XVI, and pushing him toward policies that were seen as detrimental to the well-being of the French people.

Rumours of affairs:

The queen's personal life and rumoured affairs also became subjects of public scrutiny and gossip, further eroding her public image. Rumours of her apathy and the alleged statement "Let them eat cake" when informed about the bread shortages showcased her disconnect from the everyday struggles of the French population.

Marie Antoinette's influence as a long-term cause of the French Revolution lies in the way she embodied the stark contrast between the opulence enjoyed by the monarchy and the dire living conditions experienced by most of the French population. Her actions and reputation created resentment, further fuelling the desire for political and social change.

In conclusion, Marie Antoinette's role in the long-term causes of the French Revolution cannot be understated. As the queen of France, her extravagant lifestyle, perceived interference in politics, and detachment from the struggles faced by the people contributed to the growing discontent and desire for change. The public's resentment towards her and the monarchy played a significant role in the eventual overthrow of the monarchy and the radical shifts that defined the French Revolution.

Long-Term Causes: the reasons for and extent of financial problems

"Mo Money, Mo Problems" - The Notorious B.I.G.

Lavish Palace of Versailles: Marie Antoinette and the royal court resided in the opulent Palace of Versailles, which was an emblem of luxury and excess. The cost of maintaining the palace was exorbitant, accounting for about 6% of the annual state budget at the time.

What do you think about the Palace of Versailles?

The financial problems experienced by France in the late 18th century played a significant role as a long-term cause of the French Revolution. The extent and consequences of these economic issues deeply impacted the political and social landscape, fuelling discontent and contributing to the revolutionary fervour that swept across the nation.

However, it is important to note, Louis XVI did not start the construction of the palace. It was inherited to him. The Palace of Versailles, located near Paris, France, holds a rich and illustrious history. Originally a hunting lodge built by Louis XIII in the early 17th century, it was transformed into a grand palace by his son, Louis XIV, also known as the Sun King. Louis XIV envisioned Versailles as a symbol of his absolute power and authority. The palace became the seat of the French government and the residence of the royal court, attracting the most influential and noble figures of the era.

Versailles underwent numerous expansions and renovations, gradually transforming into a masterpiece of architecture and design. Its iconic Hall of Mirrors, opulent gardens, and grand apartments showcased the lavish lifestyle of the French monarchy. The palace served as a powerful tool of propaganda, projecting the grandeur and prestige of the Bourbon dynasty to both the French people and foreign dignitaries.

Louis XVI

In 1774, the palace was inherited by Louis XVI, who ascended the throne at the age of 19. However, his reign coincided with a period of political and financial instability in France. As the financial crisis deepened, public discontent grew, and the extravagant lifestyle associated with Versailles became a symbol of the monarchy's disconnect from the struggles of the common people.

In the aftermath of the Revolution, the Palace of Versailles was transformed into a museum dedicated to preserving and displaying France's rich artistic and historical heritage. Today, it stands as a testament to the grandeur and failure of the monarchy.

Did you know?

Despite France having no monarchy, the Palace of Versailles and the Louvre are the most visited royal palaces in the world!

This is going over material already in the book, but it is important to compile this all in one place. One of the primary reasons for the financial problems in France was the extravagant spending of the monarchy, particularly under King Louis XVI and his queen, Marie Antoinette. The lavish lifestyle and opulent court at Versailles incurred immense costs, draining the treasury and burdening the French people with heavy taxation. This financial mismanagement, coupled with a lack of fiscal reforms, led to a mounting debt crisis that the monarchy struggled to address effectively.

Furthermore, France's involvement in various wars, such as the Seven Years' War and the American Revolutionary War, further exacerbated the financial strain. The cost of maintaining a powerful military and supporting foreign campaigns placed an enormous burden on the already strained economy. The government's attempts to finance these wars through borrowing and increased taxation only deepened the crisis, placing the burden disproportionately on the lower classes.

The regressive taxation system of the Ancien Régime also contributed to the growing resentment among the common people. The Third Estate, consisting of the majority of the population, bore the brunt of the tax burden while the nobility and clergy enjoyed exemptions and privileges. This stark inequality further fuelled social unrest and a desire for change.

The economic hardship faced by the lower classes was exacerbated by a series of poor harvests and food shortages, causing widespread hunger and suffering. The rising cost of bread, a staple food for the majority, created severe hardships and intensified social tensions. As the economic disparity between the privileged few and the struggling masses grew, so did the demand for reforms that would address the financial inequities and provide relief for the suffering population.

The financial problems in France were a catalyst for the questioning of the established order and the demand for change. The mounting debt, heavy taxation, and economic inequalities all contributed to a sense of frustration and injustice among the people. This dissatisfaction, coupled with Enlightenment ideas of equality and individual rights, laid the groundwork for the revolution and ultimately erupted in the French Revolution.

In conclusion, the financial problems experienced by France were a crucial long-term cause of the French Revolution. The excessive spending of the monarchy, the costs of war, regressive taxation, and economic hardships faced by the lower classes all created a climate of discontent and inequality. The quest for economic stability and relief from financial burdens played an important role in shaping the revolutionary aspirations of the French people, leading to monumental events that would forever change the course of history.

Long-Term Causes: the policies of Necker

"The financial situation of France is dire, and if left unaddressed, it may lead to disastrous consequences for the monarchy." - Jacques Necker, Finance Minister of France (1781)

In the complex tapestry of events leading up to the French Revolution, one figure stands out for his influential policies and the profound impact they had on the long-term causes of this historic upheaval. Jacques Necker, a Swiss-born finance minister, played a significant role in shaping the economic landscape of France and inadvertently contributed to the social and political tensions that would ultimately spark the revolution.

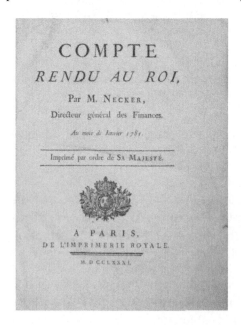

Necker's policies were driven by a sincere desire to address the pressing financial crisis that plagued France in the late 18th century. He recognized the need for fiscal reforms and implemented measures aimed at stabilizing the country's economy. Necker introduced some transparency in financial reporting, publishing detailed accounts of state finances known as the Compte Rendu. This publication was intended to garner public trust and confidence by providing a clear picture of government spending.

One aspect of Necker's Compte Rendu that angered the French public was his manipulation of financial data to present a more optimistic picture. Necker intentionally concealed some of the country's debts and financial deficits, leading to accusations of dishonesty and further eroding public trust in the monarchy.

However, while Necker's policies may have seemed well-intentioned, they had unintended consequences. The Compte Rendu, despite its transparency, highlighted the lavish spending of the French court, including the exorbitant expenses incurred by Marie Antoinette.

This revelation further drove public resentment towards the monarchy and the perception of their detachment from the struggles faced by ordinary citizens.

The publication inadvertently exposed the vast disparities in wealth distribution, further driving discontent among the lower classes who bore the brunt of heavy taxation.

Furthermore, Necker's policies, although attempting to address the financial crisis, failed to address the structural issues that perpetuated economic inequality. His reforms largely targeted taxation, burdening the peasantry and the urban poor while sparing the nobility and clergy. The debates recorded in Compte Rendu also focused on economic issues, such as price controls and food shortages.

One crazy fact is that it became an instant bestseller, selling out within days and causing a frenzy among the public. This demonstrated the French people's hunger for information about the state of the nation's finances.

The public often grew frustrated and angered by discussions that failed to address their immediate needs and worsened their economic conditions.

This unequal distribution of the tax burden intensified social grievances and deepened the divide between the privileged few and the struggling masses.

Necker's approach also faced opposition from powerful factions within the nobility and court, who resisted any attempts to curtail their privileges and influence. The clash between the old feudal order and the need for economic reforms created a volatile atmosphere that set the stage for revolutionary sentiments to take hold.

In conclusion, while Jacques Necker's policies were rooted in a genuine desire to address the financial crisis in France, they inadvertently exacerbated the socio-economic tensions that underpinned the long-term causes of the French Revolution. The publication of the Compte Rendu exposed the inequalities and excesses of the monarchy, fuelling discontent among the lower classes. The failure to implement comprehensive and equitable economic reforms further deepened social divisions. Thus, Necker's policies, however well-intentioned, played a significant role in sowing the seeds of revolution by laying bare the stark disparities and igniting a desire for change among the oppressed masses.

Long Term Causes: the problem of poor harvests.

Everybody carry the burden of Taxes and National Debt, c.1789 (colour engraving)

The problem of poor harvests held a significant influence and played a crucial role in the long-term causes of the French Revolution. Agricultural productivity and the availability of food were fundamental to the stability of French society, but a series of poor harvests exacerbated the existing socio-economic disparities and heightened the discontent among the population.

In the years preceding the Revolution, France experienced a series of crop failures and harsh weather conditions. These poor harvests resulted in soaring food prices, scarcity of essential goods, and widespread famine. The rural peasantry, who formed the majority of the population and were heavily dependent on agriculture, bore the brunt of these hardships. Many faced extreme poverty, struggled to meet their basic needs, and were burdened by high taxes and feudal obligations imposed by the nobility.

Skyrocketing Bread Prices:

The series of bad harvests in the late 1780s led to a severe shortage of grain, which resulted in a significant increase in the price of bread. Between 1788 and 1789, the cost of bread in Paris rose by a staggering 67%.

The impact of poor harvests extended beyond the rural areas, reverberating throughout French society. Urban populations, already grappling with rising living costs, were further affected by the scarcity of food and the subsequent inflationary pressures. The working classes, particularly those in industries related to food production and distribution, faced severe economic hardships, pushing them towards the brink of desperation.

Grain Hoarding and Black Market:

In response to the scarcity of grain and fears of further price increases, individuals and merchants began hoarding grain. This exacerbated the shortage and created a thriving black market for food, where prices soared even higher. It is estimated that the price of wheat increased by 88% from 1788 to 1789.

The consequences of poor harvests laid bare the structural flaws of the Ancien Régime. The monarchy and the aristocracy, who enjoyed privileges and exemptions from taxation, were largely disconnected from the plight of the common people. Their lavish lifestyles and mismanagement of resources exacerbated the suffering of the lower classes, driving resentment and a desire for change.

In some regions, particularly rural areas, peasants struggled to obtain sufficient food for survival, leading to malnutrition and famine. It is estimated that during the crisis, the average person's daily calorie intake dropped from around 2,700 calories to just 1,800 calories.

Generally, the recommended daily calorie intake is 2,000 calories a day for women and 2,500 for men.

In 2023 the U.K.'s poorest 10% have a calorie intake of 1997.

The problem of poor harvests, combined with the broader socio-economic grievances, created fertile ground for revolutionary sentiments to take root. It highlighted the need for equitable distribution of resources, fairer taxation, and a political system that would address the concerns and aspirations of the populace. The discontent stemming from the scarcity of food played a crucial role in mobilizing the masses and galvanizing support for the revolutionary cause.

Chapter Two: Short-term Causes of the Revolution:

From Assembly of Notables to Estates General, 1787–89

The King opens the meeting of the Estates-General (May 5, 1789)

By Isidore-Stanislaus Helman and Charles Monnet

The short-term causes of the French Revolution, spanning from 1787 to 1789, were marked by escalating tensions and political unrest. In 1787, King Louis XVI convened the Assembly of Notables, a group of high-ranking nobles and clergy, to address France's dire financial situation. However, their resistance to proposed tax reforms led to their dismissal. Subsequently, the king called for the Estates General, an assembly representing the three estates of French society (clergy, nobility, and commoners), which had not been convened since 1614. As the Estates General approached, the commoners, who constituted the majority of the population and were burdened by heavy taxes and economic hardship, grew increasingly dissatisfied with their marginalized role. They demanded a fairer system of representation and the establishment of a constitutional monarchy. These short-term causes set the stage for the revolution, igniting a spark that would eventually engulf France in a wave of revolutionary fervour, reshaping the course of history.

The Assembly of Notables (1787)

What was the Assembly of Notables?

The Assembly of Notables, convened in 1787 by King Louis XVI of France, was a gathering of high-ranking nobles, clergy, and some influential members of the bourgeoisie. Its purpose was to address the pressing financial crisis faced by the French monarchy. The assembly was intended to gain support for proposed tax reforms, particularly the taxation of the nobility and clergy who were traditionally exempt. However, the Notables resisted these reforms, defending their privileged status and refusing to accept any measures that could diminish their wealth and influence. As a result, the Assembly of Notables failed to achieve its intended objectives, deepening the financial crisis and exacerbating the social and political tensions that would eventually culminate in the French Revolution.

What was its role in causing the French Revolution?

The Assembly of Notables, convened by King Louis XVI in 1787, served as a significant short-term cause of the French Revolution.

Its purpose was to address the dire financial crisis that plagued France at the time. However, instead of offering viable solutions, the Notables resisted proposed tax reforms, primarily due to their vested interests. Their opposition to the necessary fiscal changes underscored the deep-rooted resistance to change within the privileged classes of French society. This refusal to share the burden of taxation further exacerbated the economic inequalities and powered public resentment towards the nobility and clergy who were seen as self-serving and out of touch with the struggles of the common people.

The Estates General, a crucial institution in pre-revolutionary France, was beset by inherent flaws that perpetuated social inequalities and created a stark disadvantage for the commoners. The structure of the Estates General, composed of three separate estates - the clergy, the nobility, and the commoners - reflected the traditional hierarchical order of French society. However, this hierarchical framework resulted in a disproportionate distribution of power, favouring the first two estates while leaving the commoners marginalized and disadvantaged.

Firstly, the clergy and nobility, comprising the first and second estates respectively, held privileged positions within the Estates General. Their combined representation equalled that of the third estate, even though the commoners constituted the majority of the population. This imbalance ensured that the interests and concerns of the commoners were often overshadowed and disregarded, allowing the clergy and nobility to maintain their influence and protect their vested interests.

The failure of the system

The voting system within the Estates General further exacerbated the disparity of influence. Traditionally, each estate had one vote, regardless of its size.

With three estates representing different sections of society, the first and second estates consisted of only around 2% of the population, while the hardworking commoners, or the third estate, made up a whopping 98% of the population. Talk about an uneven playing field!

Consequently, the commoners' overwhelming majority translated into a situation where they possessed only a single vote, equivalent to that of the much smaller first and second estates. This unequal representation profoundly disadvantaged the commoners, stifling their ability to effect meaningful change or advocate for their rights within the political sphere.

The cherry on top of this unequal sundae was the veto power wielded by the first and second estates. If any decision didn't tickle their fancy, they could simply raise their hand and veto it, thwarting the aspirations of the commoners and preserving their interests. It was like having a big red button that said "Nope!" while the rest had to accept their fate.

The commoners were left feeling as helpless as a fish out of water! The hierarchical structure of the Estates General perpetuated the existing social disparities and contributed to the frustration and grievances of the commoners. The burdens of heavy taxation and economic hardships fell disproportionately on the third estate, while the clergy and nobility enjoyed significant exemptions and privileges. This disparity in socio-economic standing intensified the sense of injustice and inequality among the commoners, fuelling their desire for a fairer system that would reflect the realities of French society.

The failure of the Assembly of Notables to address the pressing financial issues eroded the people's faith in the monarchy and exposed the underlying tensions that would ultimately contribute to the outbreak of the French Revolution. The assembly highlighted the growing divide between the privileged few and the increasingly disenfranchised masses, acting as a catalyst for the revolution that would soon sweep across the nation.

The policies of Calonne and Brienne and their consequences

The policies of Charles Alexandre de Calonne and Étienne Charles de Loménie de Brienne, and their subsequent consequences, emerged as significant short-term causes of the French Revolution.

Calonne, as the finance minister under King Louis XVI, recognized the urgent need for economic reforms to alleviate France's severe financial crisis. In 1786, he proposed a series of measures, including tax reforms, reductions in government spending, and the establishment of provincial assemblies. However, Calonne's proposals faced opposition from the nobility and clergy, who resisted any changes that threatened their privileged status. The resistance from the privileged classes led to Calonne's dismissal.

Brienne, who succeeded Calonne as finance minister, faced similar challenges in implementing reforms. He attempted to address the mounting debt by proposing new taxes on the nobility and clergy. However, his efforts encountered resistance from the Parlement of Paris, a high court composed of nobles, who refused to register the royal edicts necessary to enforce these reforms. The refusal of the Parlement sparked public outrage and increased demands for a fairer tax system and greater representation.

The consequences of Calonne and Brienne's policies and the subsequent resistance they faced had far-reaching effects. The failure to enact meaningful economic reforms and address the financial crisis deepened public discontent and exacerbated social inequalities. The privileged classes' refusal to contribute to the country's financial burden further fuelled popular resentment against the monarchy and the existing social order. This growing frustration and sense of injustice laid the groundwork for the revolutionary spirit that would explode in the years that followed.

The Tennis Court Oath

The Tennis Court Oath (June 20, 1789), by Couder

The Tennis Court Oath stands as a pivotal moment in the French Revolution, serving as a short-term cause that ignited the flames of the revolution.

Taking place on June 20, 1789, it occurred within the context of the Estates General, a gathering of representatives from the three estates of French society. Frustrated by the political stalemate and sensing the urgency for change, the Third Estate, representing the commoners, found themselves locked out of their designated meeting room.

Undeterred, they relocated to a nearby indoor tennis court. Led by figures such as Maximilien Robespierre, they took a solemn oath, vowing to not disband until a constitution was established for the nation. This defiant act demonstrated the Third Estate's determination to challenge the existing order and its commitment to pursuing political reform. The Tennis Court Oath galvanized support and instilled a sense of unity among the revolutionaries, ultimately propelling the Revolution forward. It marked a significant departure from the traditional hierarchical structure, paving the way for further revolutionary actions and shaping the course of the French Revolution in the years to come.

The storming of the Bastille

Storming of The Bastille by Jean-Pierre Houël

The storming of the Bastille on July 14, 1789, stands as a crucial moment in the French Revolution, serving as a significant short-term cause of the uprising.

Parisians stormed the infamous Bastille prison, looking to free the prisoners held within. To their surprise, they found only seven inmates, including four forgers and three insane people. Talk about an anti-climactic prison break!

The Bastille, a fortress prison in Paris, was a symbol of royal authority and oppression, housing political prisoners and storing weapons. The event was sparked by growing discontent among the common people, who were burdened by economic hardships, food shortages, and a sense of social inequality.

As rumours spread that King Louis XVI planned to use military force against the National Assembly, a revolutionary mob gathered and stormed the Bastille in search of arms and to release the prisoners.

The fall of the Bastille marked a symbolic victory for the revolutionaries, as they triumphed over a potent symbol of monarchy's power. The storming of the Bastille further galvanized the revolutionary fervour, encouraging popular uprisings across France and leading to the escalation of the Revolution.

The Storming of the Bastille wasn't just about freeing prisoners. It was also an opportunity for the revolutionaries to get a taste of sweet, sweet revenge. They captured the governor, Marquis de Launay, and paraded him through the streets of Paris. But here's the gruesome part: when they reached the Place de Grève, a public square, they beheaded him and impaled his head on a pike.

This event highlighted the people's willingness to challenge and overthrow authority, fuelling their aspirations for liberty, equality, and a more just society. The storming of the Bastille remains an indelible moment in history, catalysing the subsequent events that unfolded during the French Revolution.

The Grande Peur

"Fear spread like wildfire, gripping the hearts of ordinary French people, as rumours of brigands and marauders terrorized the countryside." (Source: Doyle, William. "The Oxford History of the French Revolution." Oxford University Press, 1989)

The Grande Peur, also known as the Great Fear, was a significant short-term cause that played a key role in fuelling the flames of the French Revolution.

Occurring in the summer of 1789, this period of intense fear and unrest was triggered by economic hardship, rumours, and anxiety among the French peasantry. The unrest was exacerbated by political uncertainty as the Estates General met in Versailles. The Grande Peur spread rapidly throughout the countryside as peasants, driven by desperation and a sense of injustice, rose against the oppressive feudal system. Concerned by rumours of aristocratic plots and fears of famine, the peasants seized the opportunity to assert their rights and seek vengeance against the nobles. They raided manor houses, burned legal documents, and attacked noble estates.

This wave of violence created a climate of panic and insecurity among the upper classes, who feared a full-scale rebellion. The Grande Peur united the peasantry and set the stage for broader societal change, as it demonstrated the power of collective action and the demand for social justice. The fear and unrest spread beyond the rural areas and served as a catalyst, pushing the revolution into a new phase.

It highlighted the deep-rooted inequalities within French society and added to the momentum of the revolution, ultimately contributing to the downfall of the Ancien Régime. The Grande Peur stands as a stark example of the impact that fears and economic hardship can have on a society, and it serves as a reminder of the volatile forces at play during this tumultuous period of French history.

The creation of the National Assembly

The creation of the National Assembly stands as a significant short-term cause of the French Revolution, marking a turning point in the events leading up to this momentous period in history.

In June 1789, the representatives of the Third Estate, composed of commoners and middle-class citizens, grew frustrated with the unequal representation and limited influence they had within the Estates General. Sensing the urgency for change, these representatives boldly declared themselves as the National Assembly, proclaiming to represent the will of the French people.

This act of defiance challenged the traditional power structure and sowed the seeds of a revolution that would reshape the nation. The establishment of the National Assembly was not only a symbolic act but also a practical move towards achieving their aspirations.

This newly formed body sought to dismantle the absolute monarchy and create a constitutional government that would guarantee fundamental rights and ensure a fair distribution of power. The creation of the National Assembly served as a rallying point for the commoners and fuelled a growing sense of unity and purpose among the discontented population.

It paved the way for subsequent events, such as the storming of the Bastille and the adoption of the Declaration of the Rights of Man and Citizen, ultimately propelling the French Revolution into motion.

Its significance lies not only in its role as a catalyst for the Revolution but also in its embodiment of the collective voice and determination of the French people to shape their destiny.

Chapter Three: Developments 1789–92

The developments of the French Revolution from 1789 to 1792 were characterized by a series of transformative events and radical power shifts. In August 1789, the National Assembly issued the Declaration of the Rights of Man and of the Citizen, proclaiming equality, liberty, and popular sovereignty. These developments laid the foundation for a new political system and social order in France, challenging traditional institutions and paving the way for the rise of Napoleon Bonaparte.

Changes brought about by the Constituent Assembly (1789–91),

The Constituent Assembly, which convened from 1789 to 1791, played a critical role in shaping the course of the French Revolution and implementing significant changes in French society.

This assembly was formed by the National Assembly, representing the commoners. Under the leadership of figures like Maximilien Robespierre and the Marquis de Lafayette, the Constituent Assembly aimed to establish a constitutional monarchy and enact crucial reforms.

One of their most notable achievements was the issuance of the Declaration of the Rights of Man and of the Citizen in August 1789, proclaiming fundamental rights and principles such as equality before the law and freedom of speech.

The Declaration aimed to establish a set of universal principles that would apply to all individuals, irrespective of their social status or background. It proclaimed that all men are born free and equal in rights, emphasizing the concept of natural rights that should be protected by the state.

It protected various fundamental rights and freedoms, including freedom of speech, freedom of religion, and freedom of assembly. It recognized property rights and outlined principles of due process and presumption of innocence.

The assembly embarked on a comprehensive process of constitutional reform, which included the adoption of a written constitution in September 1791. This constitution limited the power of the monarchy and established a constitutional monarchy with a unicameral legislature. (A single chamber for voting.) Additionally, the assembly abolished feudalism, ending the privileges of the nobility and clergy, and introduced measures to promote religious tolerance.

However, the Constituent Assembly faced numerous challenges, including political divisions and the emergence of counter-revolutionary forces. These challenges set the stage for further radicalization and changes in subsequent stages of the Revolution.

Nonetheless, the Constituent Assembly's reforms laid the groundwork for a new political and social order in France, setting in motion a transformative period that would reshape the nation's future and inspire revolutionary movements around the world.

The flight to Varennes and its impact

The arrest of Louis XVI and his family at the house of the registrar of passports, at Varennes By Thomas Falcon Marshall

The flight to Varennes, which occurred on the night of June 20-21, 1791, had a significant impact on the course of the French Revolution. King Louis XVI, feeling threatened by the revolutionary changes taking place, attempted to flee Paris with his family to seek refuge in the eastern town of Varennes, which was under the control of sympathetic royalist forces. To evade detection, the royal family disguised themselves as servants and used the pseudonyms "Monsieur and Madame de Korff" during their escape. However, their attempt was plagued by misfortune, as their carriage broke down near Varennes, a small town located in north-eastern France. The delay allowed their identities to be discovered, and they were captured and brought back to Paris.

However, their escape was thwarted, and they were recognized and apprehended by revolutionaries near Varennes.

It gets worse, Louis left a note...

The note left behind by Louis XVI during the flight to Varennes was a declaration explaining his intentions and justifications for leaving Paris. The note, known as the "Declaration to the French People," expressed Louis XVI's concerns for the safety of his family and his desire to restore order and protect the principles of the monarchy. In the declaration, he denounced the actions of the Revolution and expressed his hope to work with the National Assembly to establish a constitution that would protect the rights and privileges of all French citizens. However, the note was ultimately disregarded and had no significant impact on the outcome of the events that followed.

The impact of this event was twofold.

Firstly, it shattered any remaining trust between the king and the revolutionaries. The flight to Varennes confirmed the suspicions of many that Louis XVI was not genuinely committed to the revolution and that he sought to undermine the revolutionary changes.

Secondly, it strengthened the resolve of the revolutionary factions who now saw the monarchy as a direct threat to their goals. This incident fuelled a growing Republican sentiment and ultimately contributed to the increasing radicalization of the Revolution. The flight to Varennes solidified the belief among the revolutionaries that the monarchy was irredeemable, paving the way for the subsequent events that led to the abolition of the monarchy and the establishment of the First French Republic.

The roles of the Sans Culottes, Girondins and Jacobins

The Sans Culottes

Idealized sans-culotte by Louis-Léopold Boilly

The Sans-Culottes played a significant role from 1789 to 1792 in the French Revolution. This term, meaning "without knee breeches," referred to the urban working-class citizens of Paris who were prominent supporters of the revolution. The Sans-Culottes consisted of artisans, labourers, and small shopkeepers who were dissatisfied with their socio-economic conditions and aspired for greater political participation and economic equality. They were characterized by their distinctive clothing, often wearing trousers instead of the knee breeches worn by the upper classes.

The Sans-Culottes were instrumental in the popular uprisings and protests that shaped the revolution. They formed militant groups and played a crucial role in storming the Bastille in 1789, marking a symbolic victory against royal authority. The Sans-Culottes also had a strong presence in political clubs, such as the Jacobin Club, where they expressed their demands for radical social and economic reforms. The Sans-Culottes exerted influence on the Legislative Assembly, advocating for policies that favoured the interests of the working class, such as price controls and the redistribution of wealth. The Sans-Culottes exerted pressure on the revolutionary government, influencing policies and pushing for more democratic measures.

The Girondins

The Girondins were a prominent political group during the French Revolution, playing a significant role from 1789 to 1792. Emerging as a faction within the National Convention, the Girondins represented a moderate and liberal voice in the early years of the Revolution. They derived their name from the region of Gironde in southwestern France, where many of their prominent members hailed from.

The Girondins advocated for a constitutional monarchy and believed in granting some power to the king while establishing a parliamentary system. They championed the principles of liberty, equality, and popular sovereignty, aligning themselves with the ideals of the Enlightenment.

The Girondins played a key role in drafting and promoting the Declaration of the Rights of Man and the Citizen in 1789. They also sought to expand the Revolution beyond France, supporting the spread of revolutionary ideas and supporting revolutions in other European countries. However, the Girondins faced opposition from other factions, such as the more radical Jacobins, who saw them as too moderate and compromising.

The Jacobins

The Jacobins played a significant role during the early years of the French Revolution from 1789 to 1792. They were a radical political club formed in 1789, named after the Jacobin convent where they held their meetings. Comprised mainly of middle-class intellectuals and professionals, the Jacobins advocated for democratic and egalitarian principles, promoting the ideals of the Revolution. Led by influential figures such as Maximilien Robespierre, Georges Danton, and Jean-Paul Marat.

The Jacobins emerged as a dominant force within the National Convention, the governing body established after the fall of the monarchy. They advocated for the rights of the common people, calling for the end of the monarchy, the establishment of a republic, and the execution of King Louis XVI. The Jacobins were instrumental in enacting sweeping political and social reforms, such as the introduction of the metric system, the abolition of feudalism, and the initiation of universal male suffrage. They also implemented measures to counter internal and external threats to the Revolution, including the creation of the Committee of Public Safety.

The Legislative Assembly (1791–92)

The Legislative Assembly, which existed from 1791 to 1792, was a significant phase in the French Revolution, marked by further political transformations and the intensification of ideological divisions. It was established following the dissolution of the National Constituent Assembly.

The Legislative Assembly consisted of representatives elected by active male citizens, marking a departure from the limited suffrage of the previous period.

It aimed to establish a constitutional monarchy, wherein the king's powers would be limited by the authority of the elected legislature.

However, the Legislative Assembly faced numerous challenges during its brief existence. The political landscape was deeply divided, with factions such as the Girondins, who advocated for moderate reform, and the Jacobins, who espoused more radical change. These divisions often hindered effective governance and decision-making. Additionally, external threats loomed over France, with foreign powers expressing concerns over the revolution's spread and seeking to intervene.

In April 1792, the Legislative Assembly declared war on Austria, triggering the French Revolutionary Wars. This decision further fuelled internal tensions and radicalized sections of the population.

Ultimately, the Legislative Assembly was dissolved in September 1792, giving way to the National Convention, which marked a more radical phase of the revolution.

The declaration of war on Austria and Prussia and its impact

"War, with its trials and tribulations, has the unique power to ignite a sense of patriotism and pride, uniting a nation like no other force can." Napoleon

France's declaration of war on Austria and Prussia in 1792 marked a significant turning point in the French Revolution and had a profound impact on both domestic and international affairs. The revolutionary government, led by the National Convention, decided to engage in military conflict with these European powers due to fears of foreign intervention and the desire to spread revolutionary ideals beyond France's borders. This decision was influenced by the belief that war would unite the French people and solidify the revolution's gains.

The Impact

The impact of this declaration was twofold. Internally, it exacerbated the radicalization of the revolution and heightened political divisions within France. The Committee of Public Safety, headed by figures such as Robespierre, gained increased authority to centralize power and mobilize the nation for war efforts. The revolutionary government introduced conscription, known as the levée en masse, which led to a large-scale mobilization of French citizens for military service. This militarization further intensified the revolution and created a sense of nationalism and unity among the populace.

Externally, France's declaration of war led to a series of military campaigns and alliances that engulfed Europe in a protracted conflict known as the French Revolutionary Wars. Initially, the French armies experienced setbacks, facing resistance from the coalition of European powers opposed to the revolution. However, as the war progressed, France's revolutionary zeal, combined with military reforms and strategies, resulted in significant victories and territorial expansion. The French forces, under the leadership of Napoleon Bonaparte, showcased their military prowess and pushed the boundaries of French influence.

Furthermore, the impact of the war on Austria and Prussia was profound. While these powers initially sought to suppress the revolution, they faced unexpected challenges on the battlefield. The French armies, driven by their revolutionary ideals, posed a formidable threat. As a result, the war exposed the vulnerabilities and limitations of traditional monarchical powers and sparked revolutionary sentiments across Europe.

Overall, France's declaration of war on Austria and Prussia in 1792 had far-reaching consequences. It accelerated the radicalization of the revolution, leading to political divisions and the consolidation of power within France. Externally, it set in motion a series of conflicts that transformed the European political landscape and challenged the established order. The French Revolutionary Wars would ultimately shape the trajectory of the revolution, culminating in Napoleon Bonaparte's rise to power and the spread of revolutionary ideals throughout the continent.

The reasons for the coup of August 1792

The coup of August 1792 was a significant turning point in the French Revolution, marked by the overthrow of the monarchy and the establishment of the First French Republic. This event was driven by a combination of factors that had been brewing for some time.

Firstly, tensions between the monarchy and revolutionary forces had been escalating since the formation of the National Assembly in 1789. The monarchy's resistance to constitutional reforms, coupled with economic hardships and popular discontent, created a volatile atmosphere.

Secondly, the external threat posed by foreign powers further fuelled the revolution. In 1792, the First Coalition of European Nations declared war on France, aiming to restore the monarchy and suppress the revolutionary movement. This external threat triggered a sense of nationalistic unity among the revolutionaries, who believed that a republic would be better equipped to defend the nation. Additionally, the radical factions within the revolutionary movement, such as the Jacobins, gained influence and called for the abolition of the monarchy.

These factors culminated in the storming of the Tuileries Palace on August 10, 1792, by armed revolutionary forces. King Louis XVI was subsequently imprisoned, and the monarchy was abolished. The coup of August 1792 marked a significant power shift, as France transitioned from a constitutional monarchy to a republic. It set the stage for more radical changes and further upheaval in the years to come, ultimately reshaping the course of French history.

Setting up of the National Convention.

The setting up of the National Convention marked a crucial turning point in the French Revolution. Following the fall of the monarchy and the establishment of the First French Republic, the National Convention emerged as the governing body of France from 1792 to 1795.

Comprised of deputies elected by universal male suffrage, the Convention was entrusted with the task of drafting a new constitution and steering the nation through tumultuous times.

It was during the Convention that the revolutionary spirit reached its peak, and significant political and social changes took place. The Convention abolished the monarchy, declared France a republic, and implemented radical measures such as the Law of Suspects, which allowed for the arrest and trial of suspected counter-revolutionaries.

It was also during this period that the trial and execution of King Louis XVI took place, further polarizing public opinion.

The National Convention saw the rise of influential figures such as Maximilien Robespierre, who played a key role in advocating for a more egalitarian society and promoting revolutionary ideals.

However, the Convention also faced significant challenges, including military threats from foreign powers and internal divisions. The period of the National Convention was marked by intense political debates, power struggles, and the emergence of different political factions, including the Jacobins and Girondins. The National Convention ultimately set the stage for the next phase of the Revolution, as it paved the way for the rise of the Committee of Public Safety and the subsequent Reign of Terror. Through its decisions and actions, the National Convention shaped the trajectory of the French Revolution, leaving a lasting impact on the political and social landscape of France.

Chapter Four: Convention and Terror, 1792–94

"Every knock on the door filled us with dread, as it could mean arrest, interrogation, or worse, a one-way journey to the guillotine. The very air we breathed was tainted with fear." (Recollections of a Bourgeois Family, 1793)

The National Convention

The National Convention, established in September 1792, emerged as a pivotal governing body during the French Revolution. Faced with internal and external threats, the Convention undertook a series of actions, reforms, and legislations aimed at consolidating power, addressing pressing issues, and enacting significant changes in the socio-political landscape of France.

Upon its formation, the Convention declared France a republic, abolishing the monarchy and ending centuries of royal rule. It proclaimed liberty, equality, and the sovereignty of the people as its guiding principles, signalling a radical departure from the Ancien regime. The Convention's first order of business was to deal with the ongoing conflicts within and outside the country.

Internally, the Convention was faced with the challenges posed by counter-revolutionary forces and internal dissension. To counter these threats, the Committee of Public Safety was established in April 1793, tasked with ensuring the defence of the Republic and preserving its revolutionary ideals. Led by figures such as Maximilien Robespierre and Georges Danton, the Committee wielded significant power and initiated a series of measures to safeguard the Revolution.

To maintain internal order and suppress counter-revolutionary activities, the Convention established the Revolutionary Tribunal in March 1793. This tribunal was responsible for trying and punishing those accused of treason or conspiring against the Republic. Its establishment marked a shift towards more centralized and coercive authority, as the Convention sought to root out perceived threats to the Revolution.

The Convention also implemented various reforms aimed at reshaping French society. To create a more equal society, it abolished feudalism, dismantling the remnants of the feudal system and the privileges enjoyed by the nobility. The lands owned by the Church were confiscated and nationalized, marking a significant step towards secularization and the separation of church and state.

In addition to these socio-political reforms, the Convention also sought to create a new legal framework. It introduced the metric system, standardised weights and measures, and implemented the Republican Calendar, which aimed to break ties with the Christian calendar and symbolize the revolutionary spirit. These reforms were intended to foster a sense of unity, eliminate the vestiges of the old regime, and build a new, progressive France.

Furthermore, the Convention faced external threats from foreign powers seeking to restore the monarchy and suppress the revolutionary spirit. It responded by declaring a policy of "national defence until the peace" and mobilizing troops to defend the Republic. The revolutionary armies, led by figures such as Napoleon Bonaparte, achieved significant military victories, pushing back invading forces and expanding the influence of the Revolution beyond France's borders.

Throughout its tenure, the National Convention exhibited a dual nature. On the one hand, it sought to establish a more egalitarian society and promote revolutionary ideals. On the other hand, it employed increasingly authoritarian measures to maintain control and suppress opposition. These actions, reforms, and legislation enacted by the Convention laid the groundwork for future developments, shaping the course of the Revolution and setting the stage for the radical changes to come.

The Edict of Fraternity

An edict is a formal decree or proclamation issued by a person in authority, typically a monarch or government official. It carries the force of law and is intended to direct or regulate specific actions or behaviours within a society.

The National Convention's Edict of Fraternity was a decisive declaration issued during the French Revolution, reflecting the revolutionary ideals of unity, equality, and solidarity among the French people. It was adopted by the National Convention on December 19, 1792, to foster a sense of brotherhood and common purpose among citizens during a time of great upheaval.

The Edict of Fraternity sought to cement the principles of the Revolution, emphasizing the idea that all French citizens were equal before the law and united in their struggle for liberty. It declared that France would come to the aid of any nation seeking to overthrow tyranny and establish a republican government. This bold proclamation was seen as a departure from traditional diplomacy and an expression of solidarity with oppressed peoples across Europe.

The edict was inspired by the Revolution. It symbolized the belief that the French people had a duty to spread the ideals of liberty and equality beyond their borders, transcending national boundaries and establishing a global community based on shared revolutionary principles. It resonated with the revolutionary spirit, inspiring hope and support among like-minded individuals and revolutionaries across Europe.

From a practical standpoint, the edict had limited impact due to the challenging circumstances faced by France during the Revolution. The country was embroiled in domestic conflicts and external wars, making it difficult to provide effective assistance to other nations seeking revolution. However, the edict did serve as a rallying cry, reinforcing the notion that the French Revolution was not just an isolated event but a transformative movement that aimed to challenge and transform the existing political and social order on a global scale.

In conclusion, the National Convention's Edict of Fraternity was a declaration of unity and solidarity, embodying the revolutionary spirit of the French Revolution. It emphasized the belief in the equality and common purpose of all citizens and expressed the commitment to support other nations in their struggles against tyranny. Although its practical impact was limited, the edict left a lasting legacy by inspiring later movements and highlighting the universalist aspirations of the Revolution.

The Trial and Execution of Louis XVI

"We are not judging a man, but a system." - Pierre Victurnien Vergniaud

"I have but one goal: to be a just king, to rule with wisdom and compassion, for the betterment of my people." – Louis XVI

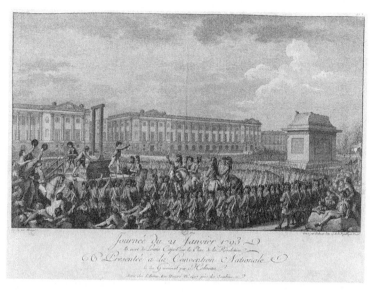

Journée du 21 Janvier 1793

The execution of Louis XVI (January 21, 1793)

The trial and execution of Louis XVI marked a decisive moment in the French Revolution, symbolizing the irreversible rupture between the monarchy and the revolutionary forces. After years of political unrest and social upheaval, Louis XVI, the last Bourbon king of France, found himself at the centre of a trial that would determine his fate.

The trial of Louis XVI commenced on December 11, 1792, before the newly established National Convention. The Convention, dominated by radical Jacobin factions, was deeply divided over the question of the king's fate. On one side, some advocated for the abolition of the monarchy and the establishment of a republic, while others believed in the possibility of a constitutional monarchy with reduced powers for the king.

The trial unfolded as a highly charged and theatrical event, with Louis XVI initially denying the authority of the Convention and refusing to plead guilty. However, he was ultimately persuaded by his counsel to adopt a more conciliatory approach. Throughout the trial, the charges against the king revolved around accusations of high treason and conspiring against the French people. The prosecution presented evidence of his alleged collusion with foreign powers and attempts to stifle the revolutionary spirit.

Despite the defence's efforts to argue for clemency and propose alternative solutions, the radical factions within the Convention, led by figures like Maximilien Robespierre, Jean-Paul Marat, and Georges Danton, pushed for the king's execution. They argued that the monarchy represented a threat to the revolutionary ideals and that Louis XVI's guilt was undeniable.

"Louis must die so that the country may live." - Maximilien Robespierre

The fate of Louis XVI was ultimately sealed on January 15, 1793, when the National Convention voted on his verdict. Out of the 721 deputies present, the majority declared the king guilty and sentenced him to death. The decision sparked a wave of intense debate and controversy, both within France and abroad.

"Though the guillotine may end my life, the principles I stand for will endure, forever etched in the hearts and minds of those who seek liberty and equality." – Louis XVI

The execution sent shockwaves throughout the continent. Louis' death not only solidified the revolutionary forces' victory over the monarchy but also intensified the domestic and international conflicts surrounding the French Revolution.

The trial and execution of Louis XVI underscored the radicalization of the Revolution and the determination of the revolutionary factions to break free from the shackles of the old regime. It represented a clear break from the past and signalled the triumph of republicanism and the abolition of monarchy in France. The event had far-reaching consequences, triggering further radicalization, foreign intervention, and the subsequent Reign of Terror.

The work of the Committee of Public Safety

"We were trapped in a state of paranoia, where friends turned on friends and neighbours became informants, all in a desperate bid to survive the relentless accusations of the Committee of Public Safety." (Diary Entries of a French Peasant, 1793)

The Committee of Public Safety emerged as an important institution during the most turbulent phase of the French Revolution. Established in April 1793, the Committee was tasked with safeguarding the revolution and protecting the newly formed Republic against both internal and external threats. Led by influential figures such as Maximilien Robespierre, and Georges Danton, the Committee exercised significant power and implemented a range of measures in pursuit of its goals.

One of the primary responsibilities of the Committee of Public Safety was to confront the mounting challenges faced by the Republic. France was embroiled in a protracted war with various European powers, and internal divisions threatened the stability of the fledgling nation. In response, the Committee implemented policies to strengthen the military, mobilize resources, and maintain order within the country. It oversaw the drafting of a levee en masse, a mass conscription of citizens into the army, which significantly bolstered France's military capabilities and ensured a steady supply of troops.

Furthermore, the Committee of Public Safety undertook an extensive program of domestic reforms. It aimed to centralize power, streamline governance, and suppress counter-revolutionary elements. The Committee introduced measures to consolidate control over local administrations, establishing a network of revolutionary committees throughout the country. These committees served as a means of monitoring and exerting influence at the grassroots level, helping to solidify the authority of the central government.

The committees favourite instrument of execution was the guillotine!

Over 16,000 people, including King Louis XVI and Marie Antoinette, lost their heads in the name of "justice." It was a gory spectacle that left the streets flowing with blood!

To combat perceived enemies of the Revolution, the Committee of Public Safety implemented a policy known as the Reign of Terror. This period, lasting from September 1793 to July 1794, was marked by mass arrests, trials, and executions of individuals suspected of counter-revolutionary activities. The Committee's justification for these extreme measures was to protect the Republic from internal enemies and maintain the revolutionary spirit. However, the Reign of Terror became increasingly indiscriminate, leading to the execution of both real threats and innocent individuals.

Despite its controversial methods, the Committee of Public Safety made significant contributions in areas such as education, culture, and public welfare. It sought to promote national unity and a sense of collective identity by introducing measures like the adoption of the Republican Calendar and the promotion of civic education. To combat food shortages and ensure a steady food supply, the Committee implemented the Law of the Maximum in September 1793. This law established price controls on essential goods, including food items, to prevent profiteering and ensure their affordability for the general public. It aimed to counter inflationary pressures caused by scarcity and speculative activities. The Committee also established government-run marketplaces, known as the "deputies of the people's stomachs," where basic foodstuffs were sold at regulated prices to ensure accessibility.

In addition to price controls, the Committee undertook measures to address the underlying causes of food scarcity. It implemented policies to encourage agricultural production, such as the abolition of feudal privileges and the division of common lands. These reforms aimed to increase productivity, encourage innovation, and dismantle traditional feudal structures that hindered agricultural progress. The Committee also supported the dissemination of new farming techniques and technologies to improve agricultural practices.

Recognizing the challenges faced by the working class, the Committee of Public Safety implemented laws to improve labour conditions and protect workers' rights. The Committee also introduced regulations to establish minimum wages, regulate working hours, and ensure safer working conditions. These measures aimed to address the exploitation of workers and improve their quality of life.

The Committee of Public Safety prioritized education and social welfare as part of its broader reforms. It implemented measures to make education more accessible by establishing free and compulsory primary schools, promoting literacy, and expanding educational opportunities for children of all backgrounds. Additionally, the Committee introduced social welfare programs to assist the poor and vulnerable segments of society, including the establishment of hospitals, orphanages, and care facilities.

The work of the Committee of Public Safety undoubtedly had a profound impact on the course of the Revolution. Its efforts to consolidate power, defend the Republic, and enact wide-ranging reforms left an indelible mark on French history. However, the Committee's policies, particularly the Reign of Terror, generated significant controversy and led to deep divisions within revolutionary circles.

Ultimately, the Committee of Public Safety reflected the complex and challenging nature of the revolutionary period. While it demonstrated the revolutionary government's commitment to preserving the ideals of the Republic and protecting it from internal and external threats, its methods and excesses also raised fundamental questions about the limits of power and the protection of individual liberties. The Committee's work serves as a poignant reminder of the complexities and dilemmas inherent in times of revolutionary upheaval.

The elimination of the Girondins

The elimination of the Girondins marks a significant turning point in the trajectory of the French Revolution. The Girondins were advocating for a constitutional monarchy and a more restrained approach to revolutionary changes. However, their political positions and increasing opposition from other factions eventually led to their downfall.

As the Revolution progressed, tensions between the Girondins and their more radical counterparts, such as the Jacobins, grew increasingly pronounced. The Girondins' moderation and reluctance to embrace radical measures often put them at odds with the more radical elements of the revolutionaries. They represented the interests of the provincial regions and feared that the radicalism of the Jacobins would undermine the stability and unity of the nation.

The Girondins also faced challenges from external forces. The Committee of Public Safety, established to address the threats to the Revolution, began to view the Girondins as a potential obstacle to their agenda. The Girondins' opposition to the execution of King Louis XVI and their refusal to endorse the radical policies of the Committee further strained their relationship with the more influential and powerful factions within the Revolution.

In May 1793, the political battle between the Girondins and the Committee of Public Safety reached its climax. The Jacobins, with Robespierre as their prominent figure, launched an offensive against the Girondins. Accusing them of being counter-revolutionary and undermining the goals of the Revolution, the Jacobins sought to eliminate their influence.

The elimination of the Girondins took place through a combination of political manoeuvring and force. The Committee of Public Safety, supported by the sans-culottes, orchestrated a series of events that culminated in the arrest and subsequent trial of Girondin leaders. Many Girondin leaders were tried and executed. Others fled or went into hiding to avoid a similar fate.

In conclusion, the elimination of the Girondins during the French Revolution represented a pivotal moment in the struggle for political power. It symbolized the triumph of radical factions, led by the Jacobins, over the more moderate voices seeking a more gradual and restrained approach to the Revolution. The events surrounding the elimination of the Girondins set the stage for the subsequent radicalization of the Revolution and the intense period of violence and upheaval that followed.

The Role of Robespierre & The Reason for and Impact of the Terror

"Power tends to corrupt, and absolute power corrupts absolutely. Great men are almost always bad men." - Lord Acton, 1887

Maximilien Robespierre, painter unknown

Maximilien Robespierre, a name that rings through the annals of history like an echo of both idealism and terror. To truly understand the role, he played in the French Revolution, we must embark on a journey into the depths of his character and the tumultuous times in which he lived.

Born in Arras, France, in 1758, Robespierre possessed a keen intellect and an unwavering dedication to the principles of justice and equality. As a young man, he studied law and quickly earned a reputation for his eloquence and passion for defending the underprivileged. It was this enthusiasm that would come to define his political career and eventually thrust him into the spotlight during one of the most turbulent periods in history.

Robespierre's rise to prominence was closely intertwined with the onset of the Revolution. He emerged as a key figure within the Jacobin Club, a political club known for its radical ideals and unwavering commitment to Republican values. Robespierre, with his piercing gaze and unwavering conviction, became the embodiment of the radical spirit that swept across France.

But it was during the Reign of Terror that Robespierre truly took centre stage, becoming both a symbol of hope for the revolutionaries and a figure of fear for those who opposed them. The Reign of Terror, a period marked by intense violence and political upheaval, was intended to safeguard the Revolution from internal and external threats. Yet, amid this chaos, Robespierre's influence reached its peak.

As a member of the Committee of Public Safety, Robespierre wielded considerable power, and it was under his watchful eye that the machinery of the Terror was set in motion. His commitment to the ideals of the Revolution, coupled with a fear of counter-revolutionary forces, led him to advocate for a ruthless approach to purging the nation of perceived enemies. The guillotine became an instrument of both justice and terror, as heads rolled in a death dance of revolution and revenge.

But let us not simplify the enigma that is Robespierre. He saw himself as the defender of virtue and the guardian of the Revolution's lofty goals. In his mind, the Terror was a necessary evil, a means to safeguard the ideals for which so many had fought and died. Robespierre believed that through the shedding of blood, he could forge a society based on virtue and equality, a society where the sins of the past could be washed away in a torrent of revolutionary fervour.

A key moment arrived with the creation of the Law of 22 Prairial in 1794. With this audacious legislation, Robespierre sought to expedite the judicial process, bypassing the cumbersome legal safeguards that had hitherto tempered the Revolution's excesses. The Law of 22 Prairial unleashed a torrent of trials and executions, as Robespierre's passion for purging perceived enemies of the Revolution reached its peak.

However, like all revolutions that lose sight of their original ideals, the Terror began to devour its own children. Robespierre once hailed as the incorruptible champion of the people, found himself facing dissent within his ranks. His uncompromising nature and growing paranoia alienated even his closest allies, and whispers of dictatorship began to circulate.

In the end, Robespierre's downfall came swiftly. His reign of terror was abruptly cut short when he faced the guillotine on that fateful July day in 1794. The man who had once embodied the revolutionary spirit had become a victim of its excesses.

So, why did the Terror take hold with such ferocity?

It was born out of a lethal cocktail of fear, paranoia, and a desperate desire for stability. France found itself besieged by external threats, surrounded by monarchies yearning to extinguish the flame of revolution. This sense of impending danger fanned the flames of suspicion within the revolutionaries themselves. No one was safe from the ever-watchful eye of the Committee of Public Safety, that fearsome body tasked with rooting out counter-revolutionaries and traitors.

But as the saying goes, "*Absolute power corrupts absolutely.*" The Committee, intoxicated by its authority, unleashed a torrent of accusations, trials, and executions. Heads rolled, quite literally, as the guillotine claimed the lives of the condemned. The noble and the bourgeois, the clergy, and the aristocrats, none were spared from its cold and impartial embrace. The streets of Paris ran red with the blood of the fallen, as Robespierre's reign of terror instilled a climate of fear and trepidation.

Let's not forget the internal strife that fuelled this grisly spectacle. France was in the throes of revolution, a nation tearing itself apart at the seams. Radical factions clashed, each vying for supremacy and their vision of a new society. Robespierre and his fellow Jacobins, staunch advocates of a virtuous and egalitarian republic, sought to cleanse France of perceived enemies lurking in its midst. In their zealous pursuit of a utopian ideal, they saw fit to purge the nation of those deemed impure, those who dared question the righteousness of their cause.

But here lies the paradox: in their quest to preserve the revolution, Robespierre and his cohorts sowed the seeds of their downfall. The Terror, once unleashed, proved insatiable. It devoured the innocent and the guilty alike, leaving no room for mercy or reason. It became a monster that could not be contained, consuming all in its path until the tides turned against its very architects. In the end, Robespierre himself met the sharp blade of the guillotine, a cruel twist of fate that symbolized the terror's self-consuming nature.

The legacy of the Terror is a stark reminder of the dangers of unchecked power and the consequences of ideological fanaticism. It stands as a cautionary tale, a dark chapter in the history of revolutions, where noble intentions are twisted into a nightmare of bloodshed and terror. May we learn from its lessons, that we may strive for change without descending into the abyss of fear and violence.

And so, my friends, as I conclude this tale of the Terror, remember that history holds within it both the brightest triumphs and the darkest follies of humanity. Let us tread carefully, with an unwavering commitment to justice and compassion, for the past has much to teach us if we dare to listen.

Impact

Maximilien Robespierre remains a figure of both admiration and condemnation, a complex character who believed that the path to a better world could be paved with blood. Whether he was a visionary or a tyrant is a question that continues to be debated. Yet, his impact on history cannot be denied. The Reign of Terror, with all its horrors and excesses, remains a cautionary tale, reminding us of the dangers of fanaticism and the fragility of the noblest of ideals.

The consequences of the Terror were devastating. Thousands of individuals, both high-profile figures and ordinary citizens, were subjected to summary trials and executed by guillotine. The fear of being accused and condemned without due process permeated French society. People lived in constant apprehension, as suspicions and denunciations became tools for settling personal scores or advancing political agendas.

The aftermath of the Terror left deep scars on the psyche of the nation. The legacy of the Terror serves as a cautionary tale, reminding us of the dangers inherent in the unchecked pursuit of power and the need for safeguards to prevent the erosion of democratic principles. It is a stark reminder that even the noblest intentions, when corrupted by unchecked authority, can lead to disastrous consequences.

The Revolution, which had begun with lofty goals of liberty, equality, and fraternity, had become entangled in a web of its own making. The once-cherished ideals were tarnished by the excessive use of violence and repression.

It left an imprint on the political consciousness of the French people, shaping their attitudes towards authority and their understanding of the delicate balance between revolution and stability.

Chapter Five: Directory and First Consul – the fall of Robespierre to the Rise of Napoleon, 1794–99

Napoleon Crossing the Alps by Jacques-Louis David.

Reasons for Robespierre's downfall and execution

"*Terror is nothing more than justice, prompt, severe, and inflexible; it is an emanation of virtue; it is not so much a special principle as it is a consequence of the general principle of democracy applied to our country's most pressing needs.*" Robespierre's Speech to the National Convention, 1794

Robespierre, a fervent advocate for the Revolution's ideals, had risen to prominence with his impassioned speeches and unwavering commitment to justice. He championed the cause of the oppressed, seeking to purge France of corruption and establish a virtuous republic. However, in his pursuit of a utopian vision, Robespierre found himself treading a treacherous path.

One of the primary reasons for Robespierre's downfall lay in the very nature of the Reign of Terror itself. The Committee of Public Safety, under his guidance, wielded immense power, acting as judge, jury, and executioner. Suspicion ran rampant, as anyone perceived as a threat to the Revolution could find themselves accused, condemned, and sentenced to the guillotine. This excessive use of state-sanctioned violence carried out in the name of preserving the Revolution, began to breed fear and dissent within the ranks of Robespierre's comrades.

Robespierre's uncompromising nature and unwavering pursuit of virtue also contributed to his downfall. He became consumed by his self-righteousness, intolerant of any dissenting voices or even perceived deviation from his vision. The once-ardent defender of freedom of speech and expression now sought to suppress any opposition, viewing it as a threat to the Revolution's integrity. This growing authoritarianism, coupled with his increasing paranoia, led to a fractured unity among the revolutionary leaders and eroded support for Robespierre himself.

VUE DE LA MONTAGNE ELEVEE AU CHAMP DE LA REUNION
pour la fête qui y a été célébrée en l'honneur de l'Etre Suprême le Decadi 20 Prairial de l'an 2 de la République Française.

Engraving celebrating the Cult of the Supreme Being

Furthermore, Robespierre's attempt to establish a new religion, the Cult of the Supreme Being, raised eyebrows and intensified concerns among his fellow revolutionaries. This deification of the state and attempts to impose a new moral order ran counter to the principles of liberty and reason that had fuelled the Revolution from its inception. Robespierre's grandiose aspirations to create a virtuous society began to unravel, as many perceived his actions as an overreach of power and an infringement upon personal freedoms.

The final blow to Robespierre came with his ill-fated speech on 8 Thermidor, Year II (July 26, 1794), which turned public sentiment against him. His diatribe against alleged conspirators and his thinly veiled threats towards his colleagues in the National Convention was met with shock and outrage. Seeing an opportunity to rid themselves of a tyrannical figure, the Convention turned on Robespierre, ordering his arrest along with his supporters.

Robespierre and his associates were promptly executed the following day, marking the end of an era and a turning point in the course of the Revolution. His downfall represented a rejection of his radical policies and an acknowledgement of the need for a more balanced and inclusive approach to governance.

In the end, Robespierre's downfall can be attributed to a combination of factors: the excesses of the Reign of Terror, his uncompromising nature, his growing authoritarianism, and the alienation of his fellow revolutionaries. The French Revolution, a period of great upheaval and idealism, serves as a reminder of the perils that can arise when even the most noble intentions are driven to extremes.

The Thermidorian Reaction

On July 27, 1794 (9 Thermidor in the revolutionary calendar), a group of moderate revolutionaries, known as the Thermidorians, orchestrated a coup against Robespierre and his supporters. This marked the end of the Jacobin regime and the beginning of a new phase in the Revolution.

The Thermidorian Reaction saw a shift away from the radicalism of the preceding years. The Thermidorians aimed to restore order and stability, seeking to distance themselves from the excesses and violence of the Reign of Terror. They dismantled the Committee of Public Safety, repealed the Law of the Maximum which had imposed price controls, and sought to ease the stringent control of the state over the economy and society.

One of the key measures of the Thermidorian Reaction was the abolition of the Revolutionary Tribunal, which had acted as the primary instrument of the Terror. The new government sought to establish a more lenient and balanced approach to justice, emphasizing the rule of law and fairness in trials. Political clubs, which had played a significant role during the Revolution, were also disbanded, signalling a decline in the influence of radical factions.

The Thermidorian Reaction also witnessed a change in foreign policy. The Revolutionary government had pursued an aggressive expansionist policy, seeking to export the ideals of the Revolution and establish sister republics across Europe. However, the Thermidorians adopted a more cautious approach, focusing on consolidating power within France and stabilizing the domestic situation.

Despite their efforts, the Thermidorian regime faced numerous challenges. Economic problems persisted, and social unrest simmered beneath the surface. The Thermidorian government was accused of being too lenient toward former revolutionaries and too conservative by those who desired further change.

Ultimately, the Thermidorian Reaction marked a shift away from the radical phase of the Revolution and towards a more moderate and stable period. It demonstrated the ebb and flow of political forces during the Revolution and the challenges faced in transitioning from an era of intense revolutionary fervour to a more settled political order.

The White Terror

The White Terror was named as such due to its association with counter-revolutionary violence and the efforts of those seeking to restore the monarchy and conservative order in the wake of the French Revolution.

It was primarily driven by the fear and resentment harboured by conservative forces, including royalists, nobility, and the clergy.

During this period, acts of violence, vigilantism, and political repression were unleashed upon those associated with the Revolution and its ideals. The White Terror targeted individuals who had played active roles in the Revolution, such as former Jacobins and supporters of the Republican cause. These individuals were subjected to arbitrary arrests, imprisonments, and even executions.

One notorious example of the White Terror was the massacre in the city of Lyon in 1793. The counter-revolutionary forces, backed by the monarchy, unleashed a brutal campaign against the city, resulting in the death of thousands of individuals suspected of supporting the Revolution. This brutal act aimed to suppress any lingering revolutionary sentiments and restore the authority of the monarchy.

The White Terror also witnessed the reestablishment of censorship, the suppression of liberal and republican ideas, and the reinstatement of strict social hierarchies. Political dissent and criticism of the monarchy were met with harsh punishments, including exile and imprisonment. The aim was to silence opposition and consolidate the power of the traditional ruling class.

However, it is important to note that the White Terror was not uniformly implemented throughout France. Its intensity and impact varied across regions, depending on the strength of counter-revolutionary forces and the degree of resistance from the revolutionary factions.

In conclusion, the White Terror emerged as a reactionary response to the French Revolution, driven by conservative forces seeking to reestablish the old social and political order. It resulted in widespread violence, political repression, and the suppression of revolutionary ideals. This period serves as a reminder of the complexities and consequences that follow in the wake of societal upheaval and the enduring struggle between opposing ideologies in the quest for political stability and social change.

The setting up of the Directory, its limitations, and achievements

The Directory emerged as a new form of government, aiming to restore stability and consolidate the revolutionary ideals that had sparked the upheaval.

In October 1795, the National Convention, the governing body of the time, dissolved itself and handed over power to the Directory. This new governing body consisted of five directors, chosen by the Council of Ancients from a list provided by the Council of Five Hundred. This system of checks and balances aimed to prevent the concentration of power in the hands of a single individual or group.

The Directory sought to establish a more moderate and stable government, in contrast to the radicalism and volatility of the preceding years. Its primary objectives were to restore order, stabilize the economy, and ensure the survival of the revolution. However, the Directory faced numerous challenges from the outset. It inherited a nation grappling with economic hardships, political divisions, and external threats from foreign powers.

Economically, France faced inflation, unemployment, and a struggling financial system. The Directory implemented measures to stabilize the currency and stimulate economic growth, but these efforts were met with limited success. The government also faced challenges from political factions, with both royalists and Jacobins seeking to undermine the Directory's authority. Internal divisions and power struggles weakened the stability of the government and hindered its ability to govern effectively.

Externally, France was engaged in conflicts with various European powers, who sought to restore the pre-revolutionary order. The Directory faced military setbacks and the rise of

Napoleon Bonaparte, a young and ambitious general who would eventually play a central role in France's future.

Limitations

One of the primary limitations of the Directory was its weak executive power. The government consisted of a five-member executive called the Directory itself, but this body often lacked unity and was prone to internal divisions and rivalries. The Directors were frequently at odds with one another, resulting in a lack of coherent decision-making and an inability to implement effective policies. As a result, the Directory struggled to provide strong leadership and address the challenges facing France.

Furthermore, the Directory faced significant economic difficulties. The country was burdened by massive war debts, inflation, and a struggling economy. Despite attempts to stabilize the situation through financial reforms, the Directory was unable to alleviate these economic woes. The poor economic conditions, combined with widespread corruption and mismanagement, led to discontent among the population and undermined the legitimacy of the government.

The Directory also faced opposition from various factions within French society. Royalists sought to restore the monarchy, while radicals desired a return to the more radical phase of the Revolution. These opposing forces posed a constant threat to the stability of the government. Additionally, military leaders such as Napoleon Bonaparte, who rose to prominence during this period, often overshadowed the authority of the Directory and exerted significant influence over national affairs.

Another limitation of the Directory was its failure to address the social and political aspirations of the population. The government was seen as detached from the needs and concerns of the people. Many citizens had hoped for a more inclusive and participatory political system, but the Directory failed to deliver meaningful political reforms. This lack of representation and responsiveness further eroded support for the government and contributed to its eventual demise.

Achievements

One of the Directory's key achievements was the stabilization of the French economy. France, exhausted by years of upheaval and war, faced significant financial challenges. The Directory implemented measures to restore financial stability, such as the introduction of the assignat currency, which helped alleviate some of the economic strain. Additionally, they sought to encourage trade and commerce by signing commercial treaties with foreign powers, boosting economic activity and fostering a sense of stability.

In terms of foreign policy, the Directory pursued an aggressive stance to protect the gains of the Revolution and expand French influence. They embarked on military campaigns to secure French borders and extend their control over neighbouring territories. These campaigns, led by military figures such as Napoleon Bonaparte, not only solidified France's position as a major European power but also showcased the effectiveness of the French military.

Another significant accomplishment of the Directory was the establishment of a centralized administrative system. They aimed to streamline the governance of France by creating a network of prefects and sub-prefects to oversee local affairs. This system helped to consolidate power and maintain control over the vast territory of France. Furthermore, the Directory initiated a process of codification and standardization of laws, leading to the creation of the Napoleonic Code, which would have a lasting impact on legal systems worldwide.

The Directory also made efforts to promote education and scientific advancements. Recognizing the importance of knowledge and intellectual progress, they established the École Normale Supérieure and other educational institutions to cultivate a new generation of scholars. This focus on education and scientific inquiry contributed to a flourishing of ideas and innovations during this period.

The royalist challenge and the coup of 18 Fructidor

A significant challenge came in the form of the Royalists, those who remained loyal to the Bourbon monarchy and yearned for its reinstatement. The Royalist movement, supported by influential aristocrats and members of the clergy, aimed to roll back the revolutionary changes and revert to the pre-Revolutionary order.

As the Revolution progressed, the Royalists sought to capitalize on the internal divisions within the revolutionary government and exploit the public's disillusionment with the escalating violence and instability. They believed that a return to a strong monarchy would provide stability and safeguard their interests. Furthermore, they looked to foreign powers, such as Britain and Austria, who opposed the Revolution and sought to intervene in France to restore the monarchy.

In response to the Royalist threat, the revolutionary government took measures to neutralize their influence and protect the gains made by the Revolution. One notable event was the Coup of 18 Fructidor, which took place on September 4, 1797, as per the revolutionary calendar. This coup saw a faction of the revolutionary government, led by Paul Barras and supported by military forces loyal to the Republic, seize power and purge the government of Royalist sympathizers.

The coup aimed to dismantle the Royalist threat by purging the government of those who advocated for a return to the monarchy. Several leading figures, including prominent politicians and generals, were arrested, exiled, or removed from positions of power. This coup further consolidated power in the hands of the more radical revolutionary factions, particularly the Jacobins, who sought to protect the Republic from Royalist influence.

In conclusion, the Royalist challenge posed a significant threat to the revolutionary government during the French Revolution. The Royalists, supported by influential aristocrats and foreign powers, sought to restore the monarchy and reverse the gains made by the Revolution. The Coup of 18 Fructidor was a important event that aimed to counter the Royalist threat by purging the government of their sympathizers. However, the struggle between the Royalists and the Revolution continued, underscoring the ongoing tensions and complexities of this transformative period in French history.

The Reasons for the Fall of the Directory

The fall of the Directory marked a significant turning point in the history of post-Revolutionary France.

One of the primary reasons for the fall of the Directory was its inherent weakness and instability. The government structure of the Directory relied on a five-man executive known as the Directory itself, along with a bicameral legislature. This arrangement was meant to prevent the concentration of power, but in practice, it led to frequent deadlock and a lack of decisive leadership. The Directory struggled to address pressing issues such as economic instability, political corruption, and rising prices, further eroding its credibility and popular support.

Furthermore, the Directory faced opposition from various political factions, each vying for power and influence. The Jacobins, who had dominated the preceding Committee of Public Safety, opposed the moderate stance of the Directory and sought to reinstate a more radical regime. Additionally, royalist factions aimed to restore the monarchy, while military leaders and generals, such as Napoleon Bonaparte, were gaining popularity and influence, further destabilizing the political landscape.

Externally, the Directory faced military challenges that further weakened its position. France was engaged in various wars and conflicts, both with neighbouring powers and within its territories. The military defeats suffered by the French army, such as the loss of territories in Italy and the failure of the Egyptian campaign, reflected poorly on the Directory's ability to protect the nation's interests and maintain its influence abroad.

Amidst these internal and external challenges, popular discontent grew. The economic hardships faced by the general population, including high taxes and inflation, fuelled frustration and a sense of injustice. Widespread corruption and a perception of elitism within the Directory further alienated the French citizens, leading to a loss of trust in the government.

In this climate of unrest and disillusionment, a coup d'état led by Napoleon Bonaparte in 1799 brought an end to the Directory. This marked the rise of the Consulate and paved the way for Napoleon's eventual ascension to power as Emperor of the French.

Napoleon's Coup

On that fateful day of 18 Brumaire (November 9, 1799), Bonaparte orchestrated a meticulously planned coup d'état, deploying his loyal troops to seize control of key institutions and dissolve the existing government. The Directory was swiftly dismantled, and in its place emerged the Consulate, with Bonaparte as First Consul, wielding immense power and authority.

Thus, the coup d'état of 18 Brumaire, and the subsequent rise of the Consulate, propelled Napoleon Bonaparte to the zenith of political power. The events that unfolded during this period would shape the course of French history and leave an indelible mark on the world stage. The era of the Consulate, with Napoleon at its helm, symbolized a significant departure from the ideals of the Revolution, heralding a new era of strong centralized authority and military might, laying the foundation for the Napoleonic era that was to follow.

In conclusion, the fall of the Directory can be attributed to a combination of internal weaknesses, political factionalism, military challenges, and widespread disillusionment among the French populace. The inability of the Directory to address the nation's pressing issues and the erosion of its popular support ultimately led to its downfall, setting the stage for a new chapter in French history under the leadership of Napoleon Bonaparte.

Napoleon Bonaparte named "First Consul."

"I was not born to be a mere mortal; destiny has named me to be more. The title 'First Consul' is but a stepping stone on my path to greatness." Napoleon

Timeline of Napoleon's Rise to Power:

1769: Napoleon Bonaparte is born on August 15 in Corsica, a French territory.

1784: Napoleon enters the École Militaire in Paris, where he receives military training.

1793-1794: During the French Revolution, Napoleon gains recognition for his military skills and rises through the ranks. He successfully defends the French government against counter-revolutionary forces in Toulon, earning him the rank of brigadier general at the age of 24.

1796: Napoleon leads the French army in Italy, winning a series of decisive victories against the Austrian forces. His successful campaigns in Italy make him a national hero and establish his reputation as a brilliant military strategist.

1797: Napoleon signs the Treaty of Campo Formio, securing territorial gains for France and strengthening his reputation as a skilled negotiator.

1798-1799: Napoleon launches an expedition to Egypt with the intention of undermining British interests in the region. Though the campaign ultimately ends in failure,

Napoleon successfully presents himself as a heroic figure through propaganda, emphasizing his accomplishments and downplaying the setbacks.

During his Egyptian campaign, Napoleon's forces discover the Rosetta Stone, a significant artifact that would later lead to the decipherment of Egyptian hieroglyphs. The Scientists and Academics that Napoleon takes with him to Europe helped cement the idea that Napoleon is a man of the Revolution and Enlightenment.

1799: Napoleon returns to France from Egypt, leaving his army behind. He capitalizes on the discontent with the Directory and presents himself as a saviour of France, appealing to the people's desire for stability and order.

1799: Napoleon publishes the "Bulletin de la Grande Armée," a military newspaper used as propaganda to spread his achievements and maintain public support.

November 9-10, 1799: Taking advantage of political instability in France, Napoleon stages a coup d'état known as the 18 Brumaire. With the help of his brother Lucien and political allies, he overthrows the Directory and establishes the Consulate. Napoleon becomes the First Consul, effectively the ruler of France.

1799: Napoleon issues the Constitution of the Year VIII, consolidating his power and establishing the Consulate as the new government system in France.

Napoleon

After seizing power in a coup d'état in November 1799, Napoleon Bonaparte embarked on a remarkable political journey that would forever alter the course of French history. The culmination of his rise to power came with his appointment as the "First Consul" in France. This new position marked a significant departure from the previous governing structures and represented a consolidation of authority in the hands of one individual.

Napoleon's appointment as First Consul was formalized through the Constitution of the Year VIII, which was ratified in December 1799. Under this constitution, executive power was vested in three consuls, with Napoleon holding the most influential position. While the other two consuls were initially envisioned as checks on his authority, Napoleon skilfully manoeuvred to centralize power in his own hands.

As First Consul, Napoleon exercised broad control over the government and implemented a series of sweeping reforms. He reorganized the administration, judiciary, and military, streamlining their operations and enhancing efficiency. Moreover, he initiated several measures aimed at stabilizing the economy, such as introducing a new currency and implementing key financial reforms.

One of Napoleon's notable achievements as First Consul was the signing of the Concordat with the Catholic Church in 1801. This agreement aimed to resolve the long-standing conflict between the Church and the revolutionary government. It reestablished Catholicism as the dominant religion in France while also recognizing religious freedom for other faiths. This conciliatory approach helped to restore order and stability, garnering support for Napoleon's regime.

In 1802, a plebiscite (A referendum) held amongst the French citizens, ratified a constitutional amendment that declared Napoleon First Consul for life. This further solidified his position and provided him with a degree of legitimacy. Napoleon, ever the master of propaganda, skilfully cultivated an image of himself as a champion of stability and order, effectively utilizing his charisma and popularity to strengthen his rule.

Ultimately, Napoleon's ascendancy to the position of First Consul marked a crucial turning point in French history. His consolidation of power and implementation of wide-ranging reforms set the stage for his later proclamation as Emperor of the French. While his rule as First Consul brought stability and significant changes to France, it also foreshadowed the growing concentration of power in a single individual—a trend that would have profound implications for the future of the nation and Europe as a whole.

Achievements of the Revolution in France (1789–99)

"The French Revolution is the most important event in the history of the world." - Thomas Carlyle

"The French Revolution was a masterstroke of bourgeois self-interest disguised as a triumph of Enlightenment principles." - Simon Schama

"The French Revolution was the focal point of an age intoxicated with the idea of progress." - François Furet

"The French Revolution represents the most colossal attempt to create social and political order by radical means in the whole history of Western civilization." - Eric Hobsbawm

"The French Revolution marked a turning point in human history, unleashing a wave of transformative ideas that continue to shape the world today." - Marisa Linton

The French Revolution, spanning from 1789 to 1799, was a transformative period in French history, marked by significant achievements that shaped the nation and reverberated throughout the world. This chapter in history witnessed a tumultuous journey from the crumbling Ancien Régime to the establishment of a new political and social order. Let us delve into the achievements of the Revolution, which continue to captivate historians and scholars to this day.

One of the foremost achievements of the Revolution was the abolition of the monarchy and the establishment of a republic. The revolutionaries, driven by the ideals of liberty, equality, and fraternity, overthrew King Louis XVI and his queen, Marie Antoinette, dismantling the oppressive and hereditary rule of the monarchy. The establishment of a republic paved the way for a more inclusive and participatory political system, wherein the citizens had the right to elect representatives and have a say in the governance of the nation.

The Revolution also brought about profound social changes. Feudalism, a relic of the past, was abolished, dismantling the oppressive hierarchy that had long burdened the peasantry. The concept of egalitarianism gained momentum, emphasizing the equal rights and opportunities of all individuals, irrespective of their social background or birthright. The revolutionaries sought to create a society where merit and talent determined one's status, challenging the entrenched privileges of the nobility.

Another notable achievement of the Revolution was the codification of laws. The revolutionary government sought to create a uniform legal system that would be fair and accessible to all citizens. This led to the creation of the Napoleonic Code, a comprehensive set of laws that outlined civil rights and liberties, provided a framework for governance and promoted the idea of a modern and egalitarian legal system.

The Revolution also witnessed significant strides in education and intellectual progress. The establishment of the Committee on Public Instruction led to the creation of a more accessible and standardized education system. Schools and universities were opened to a wider section of society, promoting literacy and knowledge dissemination. Intellectual and scientific advancements flourished, as the Revolution encouraged critical thinking, questioning of traditional norms, and the pursuit of new ideas.

Economically, the Revolution brought about changes aimed at breaking the monopolies held by privileged groups. The revolutionaries sought to dismantle the mercantilist system and promote free trade. They abolished internal tariffs and introduced measures to stimulate economic growth, such as the nationalization of church lands, which were then sold to boost the economy.

The French Revolution's achievements were not limited to the confines of France alone. Its ideals and struggles inspired people across the globe, igniting nationalist movements and sparking demands for democracy, liberty, and equality. The Revolution's impact reverberated throughout Europe, leading to political and social transformations in other countries.

In conclusion, the achievements of the French Revolution were profound and far-reaching. From the establishment of a republic and the abolition of feudalism to the codification of laws and advancements in education and intellectual thought, the Revolution transformed the political, social, and cultural fabric of France. Its ideals continue to shape the discourse on democracy, human rights, and social justice. The French Revolution remains a momentous chapter in history, demonstrating the power of ideas and the ability of determined individuals to challenge the status quo and redefine the course of a nation.

Epilogue/Conclusion

As we conclude our journey through the captivating tapestry of the French Revolution, dear reader, let us reflect on the key highlights that have unfolded before our eyes. From the prelude of life in France before the revolution, characterized by opulence and inequality, to the long-term causes such as poor harvests that fuelled the flames of discontent. We witnessed the rise of influential figures like Maximilien Robespierre, who passionately championed justice, and the impact of the Terror, a cautionary tale of unchecked power.

Now, armed with this knowledge, it is time to act and pave the path to success in your IGCSE Edexcel history exam. Here are the action steps that will lead you to triumph. First, immerse yourself in the wealth of historical accounts, delving into textbooks and reputable sources to deepen your understanding. Second, engage in critical analysis, examining the causes and consequences of the French Revolution and the significance of key figures. Third, practice your essay writing skills, crafting concise and coherent responses that demonstrate your comprehension and analytical prowess. Finally, stay curious, ask questions, and seek additional resources to expand your knowledge beyond the confines of the exam syllabus.

By following these action steps, you will not only enhance your chances of achieving a high grade but also develop a profound appreciation for the complexities of history. The French Revolution teaches us about the power of ideas, the dangers of unchecked authority, and the enduring struggle for justice and equality. So, my dear reader, embrace this opportunity, seize the reins of your academic journey, and let the transformative lessons of the French Revolution shape your understanding of the past and guide your steps into a brighter future.

Bibliography

Furet, F. (1996). Interpreting the French Revolution. Cambridge, UK: Cambridge University Press.

Hobsbawm, E. J. (1962). The Age of Revolution: Europe 1789-1848. New York, NY: Vintage Books.

Linton, M. (2006). Choosing Terror: Virtue, Friendship, and Authenticity in the French Revolution. Oxford, UK: Oxford University Press.

Mignet, F. A. (1824). History of the French Revolution, from 1789 to 1814. London, UK: Longman, Rees, Orme, Brown, and Green.

Palmer, R. R. (1959). Twelve Who Ruled: The Year of the Terror in the French Revolution. Princeton, NJ: Princeton University Press.

Schama, S. (1989). Citizens: A Chronicle of the French Revolution. New York, NY: Vintage Books.

Soboul, A. (1975). The French Revolution, 1787-1799: From the Storming of the Bastille to Napoleon. New York, NY: Random House.

Tackett, T. (1996). Becoming a Revolutionary: The Deputies of the French National Assembly and the Emergence of a Revolutionary Culture (1789-1790). Princeton, NJ: Princeton University Press.

Thompson, J. M. (1959). The French Revolution. Oxford, UK: Basil Blackwell.

Woloch, I. (1990). The New Regime: Transformations of the French Civic Order, 1789-1820s. New York, NY: Norton.

Printed in Great Britain
by Amazon

36561178R00037